PENGUIN BOOKS

Family Food

'An eye-opening approach to what little angels should eat' *Daily Mirror*

'There's something admirably refreshing about his willingness to experiment with food, and to test the worth of age-old culinary lore through a mixture of theory and practice' Victor Lewis-Smith, *Evening Standard*

'*Family Food* is a welcome antidote to the funny-face school of cookery' *The Times*

'Informative and peppered with tips' *Daily Telegraph*

'The guiding principle is utter deliciousness via scientific method. His consideration of how, why and what we cook can be understood in *Family Food*. A great present' *Evening Standard*

'This is a book to get all the family involved in cooking . . . Heston is a genius in his restaurant *The Fat Duck* at Bray. However, luckily for his readers this book is not as complicated as his restaurant food, and it provides us with great recipes that we can all get involved in' Antony Worrall Thompson, *Daily Express*

'*Family Food* is the best I've ever read on getting children into the kitchen. Give this as a present to any over-stressed parents and I swear they'll be thanking you forever more' Tom Parker Bowles, *Night & Day Magazine*

'Heston Blumenthal is a genuinely talented chef, both intuitive and innovative in the kitchen . . . To its credit, [*Family Food*] offers adult tastes and techniques that children will find very exciting . . . His recipes work, some with thrillingly simple ease . . . Blumenthal's food and ideas are vital and stimulating . . . deserves to be a bestseller – *Family Food* is a treasure-trove of useful dishes, sensibly and sensitively explained' *Time Out*

'Heston Blumenthal has produced a book imbued with culinary intelligence and good taste . . . Blumenthal has tempered his considerable technical knowledge . . . which means your average punter will have no problem following the recipes . . . *Family Food* is a top cookery book – thoughtful, provocative and above all, full of common sense' Bruce Poole, chef-proprietor of *Chez Bruce* in London, *Caterer & Hotelkeeper*

'*Family Food* bears the hallmark of [Blumenthal's] thoughtful, measured and quirky approach to cuisine . . . the recipes are interesting and easy for children' Caroline Boucher, *Observer*

'*Family Food* is a sure candidate for recipe book of the year' *Independent on Sunday*

'Blumenthal is on a mission to teach our kids (and their parents) that cooking can be fun and that the results are tastier and healthier than junk and fast food. This is sure to gain many grateful fans' *Bookseller*

'Heston Blumenthal is by far the most innovative and original chef I have ever come across' Egon Ronay

'This is a chef to be cherished' Matthew Norman, *Sunday Telegraph*

'Rumoured to be the best chef in Britain' *Guardian*

'Every once in a while a true original comes along, and Heston Blumenthal is one of these rare people. He is a chef who puts the fun in fundamental, playing with ingredients with a combination of childlike innocence, professional artistry, and real insight into food's potential, untapped before he came along' Jim Ainsworth

'Heston Blumenthal is doing what no one else in the country can manage. He makes food that is genuinely exciting to eat, and genuinely delicious. No, it's more than delicious – it's sensational' Matthew Fort, *Guardian*

ABOUT THE AUTHOR

Fast becoming recognized as one of the best chefs in Britain, Heston Blumenthal is the chef-proprietor of *The Fat Duck* restaurant in Bray, Berkshire. In 2002 he was awarded his second Michelin star and was also awarded the *Good Food Guide's* Chef of the year and the *AA Guide's* Restaurant of the Year. He is married with three children. This is his first book.

Family Food

A New Approach to Cooking

HESTON BLUMENTHAL

PENGUIN BOOKS

PENGUIN BOOKS

Published by the Penguin Group
Penguin Books Ltd, 80 Strand, London WC2R 0RL, England
Penguin Putnam Inc., 375 Hudson Street, New York, New York 10014, USA
Penguin Books Australia Ltd, 250 Camberwell Road,
Camberwell, Victoria 3124, Australia
Penguin Books Canada Ltd, 10 Alcorn Avenue, Toronto, Ontario, Canada M4V 3B2
Penguin Books India (P) Ltd, 11 Community Centre,
Panchsheel Park, New Delhi – 110 017, India
Penguin Books (NZ) Ltd, Cnr Rosedale and Airborne Roads,
Albany, Auckland, New Zealand
Penguin Books (South Africa) (Pty) Ltd, 24 Sturdee Avenue,
Rosebank 2196, South Africa

Penguin Books Ltd, Registered Offices: 80 Strand, London WC2R 0RL, England

www.penguin.com

First published by Michael Joseph 2002
Published in Penguin Books 2004
2

Copyright © Heston Blumenthal, 2002
Photographs copyright © Jenny Zarins, 2002

The moral right of the author has been asserted

Set in 9.5/14.5pt Stone Serif
Typeset by Rowland Phototypesetting Ltd, Bury St Edmunds, Suffolk
Printed in Spain

A CIP catalogue record for this book is available from the British Library

For Susanna, Jack, Jessica and Joy

Contents

Acknowledgements

Having written every word, cover to cover, of this book, other things have had to give a little; well, sometimes quite a lot! Thanks should go first to the people who have had to put up with the most. My wife Susanna has without doubt been the driving force. I can't think of many women who would have been as supportive and as strong. She really has been one of the main reasons for the success of the Fat Duck.

I would like to thank Nigel Sutcliffe, for his anchor role in the dining-room, and my head chef, Garrey Dawson, for his relentless drive for the cause, supported by Ashley Watts, Derek Creagh and the whole team at the Fat Duck. They have all had to put up with my numerous lists and eccentricities.

Thanks to Roisin Wesley, my assistant, for organizing my life at work and collating the numerous documents involved in this book.

I am greatly indebted to my friends Dr Peter Barham from Bristol University and Professor Anthony Blake from Firmenich for their tireless support, advice and inspiration. There are many brilliant academics who have supported and influenced me over the last couple of years, including Dr Alan Parker and François Benzi at Firmenich, Dr Len Fisher at Bristol University, Dr Tom Coultate, Joachim Schafheitle, and 'Mr Ice Cream', Robin Weir. And to Hervé This, the chemist who is changing the way that the French are thinking about their food.

I don't know whether to thank or blame Harold McGee for

inspiring me some fifteen years ago with his brilliant book *On Food and Cooking: The Science and Lore of the Kitchen*. He continues to inspire.

Thanks to Raymond Blanc for giving me the chance years ago and passing on some of his passion. Thanks to Michel Roux for all his support in the early days. I particularly want to thank my old friend, Marco Pierre White. His kindness and generosity from the day we first met in 1984 is second to none and his contribution to British gastronomy immeasurable.

The villagers of Bray need a special mention: their support over the last couple of years has been vital. In particular, thanks to Ron Tillian, Alwyn Jones, Norman and Anne Williams, Lindsay Bailey, Dr John Sedgewick, Pauline and David Sleeman, Helen and Stephen Palmer, Ian Prosser and anyone else that I have forgotten.

Deepest thanks to Matthew Fort, Egon Ronay and Jay Rayner for their unequivocal support, sometimes in the face of criticism. I would also like to thank Felicity Dahl, Maureen Mills at Network London, Fiona Lindsay and Linda Shanks at Limelight, Aku Patel and Cyril Alfille.

Thanks to the people at Penguin: Lindsey Jordan, for putting up with me trying to write a book while running a restaurant, John Hamilton, Annie Lee, the photographer Jenny Zarins and the designer Craig Burgess.

Thanks to Nick Wilson. Without him this book would not exist.

Finally, thanks to my parents, Stephen and Celia, for everything they have done for me.

Introduction

Yet another book on children's food? It seems to be the flavour of the month at the moment. Almost every week there is a new book aimed at getting children to eat a wider variety of foods. Many of these books show how to make a face or a train from sausages, peas and mashed potatoes or, alternatively, suggest that by serving up a plate of crudités you will be able to introduce your kids to a wide variety of new, exciting and healthy vegetables. Very often these books are based on a gimmick; enticing the unsuspecting parent with the promise of hassle-free dinners and mealtimes that look as if they are out of some 'happy parents monthly' magazine!

Processed food manufacturers are fuelling this trend in the increasingly lucrative and competitive world of children's food. Although, thankfully, the days of displays of sweets by the checkout, proving impossible to ignore, have almost gone, they have been replaced by children's food packaged to entice. Processed meats cut in the shape of a teddy bear's face and tins of 'Barbie' spaghetti are only two of the hundreds of potential purchases facing the parent who wants to get through the supermarket relatively unstressed.

I talk from bitter experience, having once returned from the supermarket with my daughters, Jessica and Joy to find my wife, Susanna, asking why I had bought half of the things I had. The children never actually ate any of these items, she said. 'They told me to buy them,' I replied, only then realizing from the grinning faces looking up at me that I had been conned.

Britain now has one of the longest working weeks in the world, with, in many cases, both partners pursuing a career. We are becoming a treadmill society in which convenience is king. The giant supermarket chains have almost taken over our domestic shopping requirements and have grown into entities so powerful that they can actually influence the way we eat. These stores do have a few major advantages. First, parking: the number of cars on our roads has increased so much that in many towns and cities parking is becoming a serious problem. A store that offers free on-site parking is a valuable time-saver, and a comparatively low stress-provider if we have children to cart around. Second, size: it is no longer necessary to go to several different shops to complete our shopping list, as everything is under one roof. In addition, the immense buying power of the big supermarkets enables them to reduce food costs and offer loss leaders in order to keep the customer in that store, with the knowledge that they will recoup the loss on other products. Couple this with smart, welcoming packaging and services ranging from baby facilities to home delivery, and it is easy to see why the big supermarket chains now dominate the market.

What has happened in many areas of the country, however, is that small local traders have been forced to close, leading to the breakdown of local communities. In London, conversely, some areas too developed for a large hypermarket to be built still have a local butcher, fishmonger and greengrocer and are subsequently more like a village community than some rural villages themselves.

The reduction of food costs that the supermarkets offer must be hailed as a positive step in some respects, as it brings a wider range of products to the lower-income consumer. However, there is a more sinister downside to this. The need for supermarkets to offer ever-decreasing prices in order to boost sales has resulted in over-farmed and over-cropped produce. One example of this is the fact that the more expensive tomatoes are labelled as being 'grown especially for flavour'! Does this mean that all other tomatoes are grown without flavour? Another is chicken – a matter of pence for a packet of six breasts. What life can these animals possibly have had? It is quite understandable that this does not occur to most people: after all, we are not farmers, so why should we know anything about meat production?

We talk about a food revolution in this country over the past fifteen or twenty years, and in some respects there have been enormous changes in foods available in supermarkets, and the quality of cooking in restaurants, particularly in London, has improved massively. Modern technology and transport methods mean that we can eat almost anything we like at any time of the year: strawberries at Christmas, peaches in March and asparagus in November are just a few examples. Food and travel are increasingly being linked on television and in magazines, reflecting our ability to buy ready-made meals from around the world in our supermarkets. We can now have an Indian evening, an East European goulash or a taste of the Orient. We can even re-create the taste of our last holiday at the press of a microwave button. Hours of television time and pages of glossy magazines are now devoted to food: picture after picture of fashionable dinner gatherings, alfresco

Sundays, with soft, cleverly angled photography – but is this just marketing veneer, a media-created fantasy world of style and living that, as individuals, we all aspire to?

I can't help feeling that to a certain extent it is exactly that: something for us to buy into, satisfying the pockets of big, mass-producing companies. Look, for example, at the advertisements for some of the huge-selling juice drinks aimed specifically at children. They show healthy, well-dressed teenagers living in an area full of greenery where the sun is always shining, rushing home from school and glugging down gallons of sun-kissed juice before darting back outside to expend all of this new-found energy. Most of these drinks are no more than glorified orange squash, produced on a large scale for a lot of profit. Somebody please tell me what is wrong, expensive or difficult about squeezing some fresh orange juice! The juice from squeezing fresh oranges will have more fibre, from the bits of orange, which is definitely better for your children, and it will not be crammed full of sugar.

Popular contestant-based food programmes risk turning cookery into a pseudo-gastronomic circus and talented chefs into their juggling clowns. Television companies are constantly searching for new angles and ideas in order to produce programmes with a high viewing rate, and it seems that the easiest way for them to do this is to come up with a new gimmick. Many cookery programmes just seem to underline our growing impatience in this high-speed society, showing us how to produce a meal in twenty seconds from the contents of someone's sports bag! On the other side of the coin, the doyenne of British cookery programmes, Delia Smith, produced a series on television which aimed to get people 'back to basics', focusing on all aspects of cooking, ranging from boiling an egg to cooking meat. A team of over twenty people worked for months on the research for the Delia Smith series. It was a stark contrast to much of the rubbish that was spilling on to our television screens, and made a genuine effort to take much of the mystique out of cooking and enable people to approach food in a far more relaxed manner.

Although in normal terms the series was popular, in Delia Smith terms it was less so, causing some controversy. Many viewers felt that they did not need to be told what simmering water looked like or how long to boil an egg for. In some respects this gives us an insight into just how far the food revolution has come. Instead of feeling insulted, we should be over the moon that we can create a delicious meal from only a handful of fantastic ingredients by respecting the ingredients themselves. It is in fact very important to understand the effects of water simmering barely, lightly, moderately or heavily. Water can only boil at one level: boiling! Below that, however, it can simmer at different levels. Different processes require different temperatures. Whether it be poaching an egg, poaching a pear, simmering a stock, braising meat or cooking potatoes, the correct information enables recipes to work and allows the cook to approach the ingredients with greater confidence.

At the Fat Duck, months are spent working on perhaps just one ingredient – haricots verts for example (which will be further explained in the vegetable chapter, page 201). Hopefully, in this book some of these results can be passed on, so that without too much trouble you will be able to rediscover the taste of good ingredients by bringing the best out of them

– and without having to resort to following some of these farcical TV programmes and coming up with such gastronomic delights as toad in the hole using a Swiss roll!

If we look at the restaurants available for us to take our children to, our options seem to be dominated by a handful of fast food outlets and big chains. And all of these have one big issue in common: they are competing for our children's business! The speed with which we live our lives seems to be constantly accelerating. It's like watching one of those films of people almost falling out of a train in the morning rush hour, only on fast forward! By offering something more than food, these places can offer that sometimes precious gift – a few stress-free minutes so that the parent or parents can relax, unwind and muster up enough energy to get through the rest of their manic day. This means, however, that we must endure second-rate, mass-produced food so that our children can do some drawing or walk away with a nice little toy. Many of these children, who of course are also subjected to this kind of food, will develop a totally misconceived idea of what a restaurant actually is.

Factor There seemed to be a need for a book that would inspire parents to involve their children in the kitchen, but not in a way that made them semi-redundant themselves – only being called in to press the button of the food processor, fold in some cream or deal with a hot pan! It would need to be a book that encouraged parents to involve their children right from the outset: choosing the dish, sourcing the ingredient and being a valuable member of the kitchen. This enthusiasm would transfer itself to the meal itself, enabling children to get more involved and, ultimately, enjoy the pleasures of the table.

To be successful, though, the book would first have to inspire the parent, and there were several ways to do this. It would need to be structured in such a way that the recipes them-selves, although important, were not cast in stone. This would be best achieved by passing on some of the techniques that we use in a professional kitchen. In this regard, you must forgive me if the text may sometimes seem very detailed. The thing is, there really is a lot of information to fit into these pages. The scientific elements will help provide the foundation while the interactive experiments dotted around the book will help to keep you and your children interested and hopefully stimu-lated to cook and experiment for yourselves. There are many chances throughout this book to make little experiments or taste tests. Please try them, as not only are they great fun, they also provide an invaluable learning opportunity that will generate real interest.

In some respects, the recipes are there to demonstrate the techniques and almost to show off the results. This way, much of the mystique is taken out of cooking and replaced by greater confidence in the kitchen. If some of this confidence can be passed on to your children it will be a fantastic asset for them – and, if nothing else, it will mean that you will be guaranteed a better meal when they eventually invite you over for lunch or dinner! You can teach them how to cook the perfect roast chicken, for example, or the principle for blanching green vegetables or making pommes purée as good as you will find anywhere.

Many of these principles may seem completely new to you, and some may appear a little long-winded at first, but once it becomes clear why the extra information is there it will make sense and the kitchen will seem much more approachable. These techniques can be adapted so that you can shop without having an exact recipe and be more confident that when you open your fridge or cupboard you can concoct something for dinner out of what is there.

To give you an idea of how important the understanding of technique is, the French chemist Hervé This, who has a Ph.D. in molecular gastronomy, has a laboratory in the Collège de France in Paris. He is, in effect, studying theories of cooking and the way we eat, dispelling or supporting new and old cooking myths, and is probably doing more for gastronomy in France than anyone at the moment. Indeed, some of his theories have crept into my cooking and this book.

Eating is the only thing we do that involves all of the senses. If we see the colour red we do not stop to question whether it is in fact that colour, because in most cases it is only our eyesight that we use to evaluate this. When we eat, however, we use all our senses. Not necessarily consciously, but we do. The process of evaluation is therefore far more complicated. Add the brain into the equation and the process becomes very complex. The genetic map that controls the brain-to-palate connection is the most complex in the body – more so than reproduction!

Many psychological and sociological factors will determine how we deal with the food that we taste. These range from the type of person we are to any preconceptions that we develop through our culture or upbringing; even our childhood memories play a vital role in whether we like something or not. Texture plays a vital part in the way that we taste our food. If we bite into an apple that is soft, it will appear old; a soft biscuit that should be crisp will appear stale before we actually taste it; cola that has lost its fizz will appear more sweet. A couple of years ago, an experiment was conducted during a wine waiters' course in Paris. Unfortunately for the students, they were not aware that this experiment was being carried out – at their expense! White wines with a definitive but not overly pronounced white wine character were coloured red with pigments extracted from red wine (non-aromatic). All the students made notes using red wine characteristics! Even the organizers, who knew that the wines had been coloured with no alteration in taste, found that the wines tasted different, such is the power of sight in affecting the way that we eat our food.

The idea of this book is to get children eating adult food and parents discovering new dishes or rediscovering ones they already knew. Without trying to sound too poetic, you will be on a journey of discovery with your children, which will be as much about spending enjoyable interactive time around the table as about the cooking and food itself.

Most of us are not aware of what actually goes on in our mouths and, in particular, whereabouts we actually taste our food. How many of you know the difference between taste and flavour, and which it is that our tastebuds actually register? To help explain this, there is a fantastic little demonstration that can be done with your children that perfectly shows where taste and flavour actually happen. All you need is a few biscuits, a little salt, and whichever small children are available! Take a biscuit each, and put the salt into a small dish.

All together, squeeze your nostrils so that no air can pass into them, take a generous bite of a biscuit and chew. Do not swallow or let go of your nostrils. You will not be able to taste anything. Now, with your nostrils still squeezed and the biscuit still in your mouth, dip your finger in the salt and put it into your mouth. You will notice now that, although you could not taste the biscuit, the salt is perfectly detectable. Finally, let go of your nostrils and wait for a couple of seconds – now the flavour of the biscuit will come through!

Basically, when we eat, the tastebuds on our tongue pick up tastes – sweet, salt, acid, bitter, umami and a few other characteristics – but do not pick up any flavours. When we eat our food, however, the flavour molecules pass up into our olfactory bulb, situated behind the nose. This is where flavour is registered. Our brain then has the difficult task of linking the two systems together. When our nostrils are squeezed together, the oxygen supply passing through the olfactory bulb is cut off, preventing it from deciphering this information.

Another test that you and the children will have great fun doing is tasting soft drinks. Take 4 glasses and fill them with cola, fizzy orange, lemonade and tonic water. Put a straw into each glass. Now blindfold the first volunteer and squeeze their nostrils together. (You could put a peg on their nose, but the pain might distract them from thinking about what it is that they can taste!) Give them random tastes from each glass and let them try to name the drink. It is quite interesting to give them the same drink a couple of times in a row. The drink most likely to be picked out will be the tonic water, because of its bitterness.

This great little exercise clearly shows the difference between taste and flavour and can really get kids thinking. It also shows why, when you have a cold, you cannot taste much and some foods seem really acidic. The acid, as with the salt, is registered in the mouth and not in the oxygen-inhibited olfactory bulb.

We've found that this is a great way to demonstrate the effect of seasoning on food; for example, I recently managed to get my son and eldest daughter, Jack and Jessica, to taste beef with and without pepper. It was almost impossible to get them to eat any food that had black pepper on it until I got them to try this test, but they are now converted.

If you're interested to know more about the subject of taste and flavour, my friend Professor Anthony Blake has written about it on page 35 of this book.

Helping children understand important techniques in food will make the kitchen a friendlier place where they will want to spend more time. This greater enjoyment means that they will come to the table with more confidence – they won't look at mealtimes as a chore but as a valuable opportunity to spend time with parents who otherwise may have been far too busy. Over a period of time you will be able to build up a repertoire of dishes that both you and your children will enjoy cooking and eating.

This, together with the fact that you'll be able to make such basics as pommes purée regular items in your fridge should make choosing what your children want to eat, and shopping for food, a lot easier and more pleasurable.

In this book some useful restaurant techniques and principles have been adapted for the home cook so that they can be applied to different dishes, not just the ones featured here. Hopefully as a result you will be able to approach other cookery books with greater confidence. On pages 41–6 you will find an extensive range of conversion charts – I've always found it infuriating being told to measure, for example, $1^1/_2$ cups of something or 2 sticks of butter!

Hygiene

Hygiene in the kitchen is paramount, and should be something that your children learn hand-in-hand with cookery itself. If they start from day one then it will become second nature for them. (See Useful Addresses, page 339.)

- Never cut cooked meats on a board that has been used for cutting raw meat.
- Use a bacteriological hand cleaner after completing each task in the kitchen – you can use it for knives and other implements as well.
- Never store raw meats above cooked food as they may drip. There is more on the subject of bacteria and meat in the Sunday lunch chapter.
- The outside of a chicken's egg, by the way, can carry a lot of bacteria, which is something that many people tend not to realize.
- Use your sense of smell. After all, if you have a knife that hasn't been cleaned properly and still smells of smoked mackerel, you won't want to slice a banana with it, will you?

Equipment and ingredients

I don't want to encourage you to go out and buy a whole new kitchen – but there are some items that will make a world of difference to you and your children.

Scales: A good set of kitchen scales is important. You should make sure that they are accurate. When my wife was testing some of the recipes, they were less than successful. She then tested the scales and found that they were OK above 150g. Below that, however, they were way out and below 100g were only 50 per cent accurate! No wonder the recipes weren't working.

Mandolin or adjustable slicer: These adjustable slicers are now quite easy to find and are relatively inexpensive. They will be well worth the investment. They are ideal for slicing vegetables very thinly for a soup, for example, where the ingredients require the shortest possible cooking time. Slicing on a mandolin for a gratin of potatoes will have two benefits. The slices will be thinner than those cut by hand, exposing greater surface area and hence flavour. They will also be of even thickness.

A word of warning, however: *always* use the finger protector provided, as the mandolin blade is extremely sharp.

Blenders: Of these, the most important types are the food processor and the liquidizer. You may have one that combines both. If you have neither, a liquidizer will probably be of greater use, especially for this book – you cannot really blend soups or juice fruits very successfully in a food processor.

Failing these, an old-fashioned vegetable mill would be good. These old-fashioned sieves actually have an advantage over their modern-day counterparts in that they leave unwanted skins behind, for example when puréeing peas.

Unfortunately, these mills have all but disappeared now.

Hand-blenders and hand-held whisks can make your life a lot easier. They also have the benefit of freeing up your other hand. Your children will become less bored when they have a spare hand to cause trouble with!

Sieves: Buying a few different sieves really does pay off. The most useful ones are:

- A flat 'drum sieve', which looks a bit like one of those gold-prospectors' bowls and is great for ridding vegetable purées of any lumps; the purée is simply passed through the mesh using a plastic scraper. They are particularly useful for making a fine and silky-textured mashed potato. You will also need the plastic scraper for this.
- A fine-meshed conical sieve is ideal for most semi-liquid foods, ranging from soups to fruit purées. To make this job even easier, buy a relatively sturdy kitchen ladle for pushing liquids and loose purées through.
- A flour sieve.
- A colander. This is a larger-holed sieve, useful for draining vegetables.
- A spider. This is a meshed spoon or spatula which is very useful for taking things like pasta and vegetables out of hot water.

Knives: A good sharp knife is essential in the kitchen. It will make the job much quicker and, believe it or not, a blunt knife is a lot more dangerous because it is more likely to slide off what you are cutting, making it less controllable.

Carving meat with a blunt knife is quite likely to squeeze the juices out, leaving the meat drier. A blunt knife will also make you cry more when you chop onions, as the cell walls containing the tear-making sulphonic acids will be damaged more.

I suggest buying 3 or 4 different knives, including a good-sized all-round chef's knife and a serrated one. Remember to sharpen them each time you use them. An old-fashioned steel is ideal for this.

Just remember, when buying a knife, to make sure that it sits well in your hand and is comfortable to hold. With cutlery, a sharp knife makes meat seem less tough, even to an adult. A child having to go through a minor arm-wrestling competition to cut through his or her meat is going to find it far less appetizing.

Bowls and things: Life in the kitchen will be a lot easier if you invest in, say, 3 or 4 stainless steel mixing bowls with rounded bases. These are much the easiest to use – stirring in a flat-bottomed bowl means that part of the contents may be left around the edge. Making mayonnaise, or whisking cream, for example, is also much more difficult in a flat-bottomed bowl.

A flexible, rubberized spatula that is also heat-resistant is a simple kitchen tool that will make life much easier. It will ensure that nothing in the bowl is left unstirred, and that when scraping the contents of a container, bowl or pan into some other receptacle, the job will be done in no time at all, leaving the bowl almost spotless. The only problem with this is that the days of licking the bowl clean may well be over!

Pans: Unfortunately, this is where the budget could be blown. However, it will pay off in the long run to invest in a few different-sized saucepans and frying pans. They will make a world of difference in terms of the quality of the end result and ease of preparation. A good-quality, heavy pan may cost a bit more, but it will be worth it in the long run as it will last much longer. Pans with handles that are ovenproof will prove to be more versatile.

Roasting trays: A roasting tray will be a great asset. It is quite important to get as heavy-duty a tray as possible, as it will be used over the heat as well as in the oven; the heavy-bottomed enamel ones are ideal. Just make sure that it will fit into your oven and that it is at least 4cm deep.

Thermometers and probes: A thermometer for measuring the temperature of liquid will be useful, particularly for puréed potatoes; look for one that is fairly sensitive to degrees Fahrenheit. An oven thermometer is essential; it is surprising just how inaccurate your oven temperature may be.

Battery-operated digital probes are relatively easy to buy now and are well worth the money. You will be able to obtain perfectly cooked meat and fish using one of these. A bonus is that your children will come to understand the principles of meat cooking a lot more easily. In effect, lean meat tissue begins to denature round about 60°C. (The same point in fish cookery happens at just above 40°C.) As the temperature rises, the fibres continue to contract, forcing out the juices. By the time the temperature has reached 70°C, the meat will start to be overcooked. Meat contains around 75 per cent water, and as water evaporates at 100°C, care must be taken that the meat does not get too hot or it will dry out. You only have to look at the size of a piece of very well-done meat compared to a piece of meat the same size cooked to around 60°C: the well-done piece will be noticeably smaller, due to the amount of juices lost.

It is important to bear in mind that these factors only apply to lean cuts of meat. Pieces or joints of meat with more connective tissue need to be cooked for much longer periods of time in order to gelatinize the tougher bits and make the meat meltingly tender.

Odds and ends:

- Muslin cloth can be very useful for straining sauces. Wet it under the cold tap, squeeze out and use double thickness. Wetting the muslin first enables it to trap more impurities.
- A good mix of spoons and spatulas will make your life in the kitchen a lot easier; try to get wooden spoons, some with a flat edge and a few slotted ones for lifting food out of liquids.
- A flexible, heat-resistant spatula is great for efficiently scraping out a bowl or stirring custard in the pan, among other things.
- A large ball of string will always come in handy.

Salt and pepper: Pepper very quickly loses its fragrance. Whenever a recipe calls for pepper, use it freshly milled.

While on the subject, salt is one of the most important ingredients in the kitchen. It is a flavour enhancer that is essential and tends to be the cause of the biggest difference between a domestic and good commercial kitchen.

You will need fine table salt and, for sprinkling over finished dishes, fine sea salt crystals. These are sold in the supermarkets as Maldon salt or, which is even better, the French fleur de sel. These are the fine salt granules that naturally occur on the surface of the sea water and are simply skimmed off. At the restaurant we use a mixture of fine sea salt as it gives an even seasoning and the French fleur de sel for its crunch and subtle sweetness.

Salt has a really important function that many of you will not be aware of: it can reduce bitterness. Many cooks and chefs will add sugar to try to reduce the bitterness of a stock or sauce, to little avail. Adding salt, however, will do the job far more effectively.

Again, there is an excellent experiment to try with the little ones to show just how salt can reduce bitterness. Pour some tonic water into a glass. Take a sip, note the bitterness and add a little salt. Taste again. Repeat this process, increasing the salt each time. You should find that the bitterness of the tonic water decreases. (There will of course become a point where the salt content has become such that the tonic water will just taste salty.)

Butter: As a rule, stick to unsalted butter when cooking as you will achieve more consistent results and the butter will be less prone to burning.

Using the book

Before using a recipe, read the whole thing through carefully first. This way, you will understand the technique involved and will approach the recipe in the right manner. With a few exceptions, the recipes in this book are relatively simple. Please do not be put off by the length of some of them. Many recipes fail due to insufficient information. I want to avoid this as much as possible. In many cases, the extra information will be invaluable for general use in the kitchen and will help you and your children to gain a greater understanding of cooking. You may also find it useful when following recipes in other books.

By reading and understanding the recipe first, you will be able to judge what equipment you might need, including the size of bowl or pan required. This is easier than me telling you to take, for example, a roasting tray say 30cm long. The exact dimensions of a pan or roasting tray, unless otherwise stated, are not vital; as long as it is not so small that the ingredients won't fit, or so large that they will be lost!

When cooking something in the oven, I would always recommend that you begin by putting an oven thermometer on the shelf that you will be using. This way, you will get to know just how accurate your oven actually is – unfortunately, even with many modern ovens, the temperature to which you have set it will not be the actual temperature inside the oven. I cannot emphasize this enough, as it is so disheartening when a recipe does not work. You may be thinking that it is something that you have done wrong, not realizing that it is actually your equipment that is at fault, whether it be, for example, the oven or a poor set of scales.

With many of these recipes, I felt there was no need to mention the more obvious aspects of preparation that your children can get involved in: for example, sieving flour or stirring a pan. The book is meant to encourage you to take a far more holistic approach to cooking, treating your child with the respect that he or she deserves. Children have an immense capacity for tasting. Just because their general level of education is not as advanced as ours, it does not mean that they have any less ability to taste.

Why on earth did parents ever tell their children to chew their food so much that it becomes devoid of any taste! Could this be linked to why children tend to chew food and move it around in their mouth forever when they do not like something, instead of swallowing it as quickly as possible? They are simply prolonging the agony. How can we expect our offspring to develop an interest in food and cooking with that attitude? Instead, we should be doing just the opposite, encouraging them to be aware of flavours and aromas and how to extract the most from ingredients. For example, when making a soup or adding fragrant herbs to dishes, smell the vapour. Unfortunately, the first aromas that you can smell tend to be the most fragrant ones, and it means that these aromatic flavours have been cooked out of the food that we will be eating. There is not always a practical way to prevent losing these flavours, but it does make us think about the ingredients more.

In several places in this book I've talked about increasing the flavour of ingredients by various methods. One simple one, which can be adapted to all areas of the kitchen, is the juxtaposition of textures. Take, for example, tarte Tatin. A little raw apple grated over the hot caramelized apple in the Tatin lifts the flavour amazingly. A few very fine slices of raw celery over braised celery will strengthen its flavour, as will some cubes of very lightly cooked butternut squash in butternut soup.

In the past year at the Fat Duck, we have really begun to broaden our horizons when looking at food. Playing tricks with foods can have a big impact at a gastronomic level, and is something that we are increasingly looking at – whether it be chocolates flavoured with pipe tobacco or caviar, smoked bacon and egg ice-cream, or being spoon-fed! We have an interesting petit-four that we serve with coffee at the restaurant – a bite-size jelly made with beetroot juice. Tartaric acid is added at the end of the cooking process and left to set. The sheet of jelly is then cut into rectangles and dipped in granulated sugar. It looks as if it is made from blackcurrant. And because the tartaric acid that is added at the end also exists in blackcurrants, the jelly will taste of this fruit. When it is served, the customer is told to think of blackcurrant with the first mouthful and beetroot with the second. It has the flavour of the one that is being thought about!

This approach to cooking is not, however, new. In his translation of the *Vivendier*, a fifteenth-century French cookery manuscript, Terence Scully gives the following two outrageously wonderful 'trick' recipes that would send shock waves through environmental health departments all over the country.

To make a chicken be served roasted. Get a chicken or any other bird you want, and pluck it alive cleanly in hot water. Then get yolks of 2 or 3 eggs; they should be beaten with powdered saffron or wheat flour, and distempered with fat broth or with the grease that drips under a roast into the dripping pan. By means of a feather glaze and paint your pullet carefully with this mixture so that its colour looks like roast meat. With this done, and when it is about to be served to the table, put the chicken's head under its wing, and turn it in your hands, rotating it until it is fast asleep. Then set it down on your platter with the other roast meat. When it is about to be carved, it will wake up and make off down the table upsetting jugs, goblets and whatnot.

To make that chicken sing when it is dead and roasted, whether on the spit or in the platter. Take the neck of your chicken and bind it at one end and fill it with quicksilver and ground sulphur, filling until it is roughly half full; then bind the other end, but not too tightly. When you want it to sing, [heat] your neck of chicken. When it is quite hot, and when the mixture heats up, the air that is trying to escape will make the chicken's sound. The same can be done with a gosling, with a piglet and with any other birds. And if it doesn't cry loudly enough, tie the two ends more tightly.

These ideas today now seem totally absurd – but absurdities exist today too. For example, why on earth would a vegetarian want to eat a soya-bean-based product made specifically to look like the very thing they will not eat, real mince?

From reading this introduction you'll notice that I feel one of the most important things to try to achieve with your children is to approach the kitchen and food with a completely open mind. This, however, will have to come first from you, the parent. Any of you that are more conservative in your approach, please try to dispel any preconceived ideas you may have. The world of cooking and eating will not be the same again.

A Note on the Flavour of Food
by Professor Anthony Blake

'Flavour' is a word which, although used routinely in conversation to describe our food, is often not very well defined nor properly understood. Although 'flavour' is a single word, it in fact describes a complex and interacting set of sensations we experience when we eat. During the simple process of taking a mouthful of food, chewing it and swallowing it, all our senses provide information to our brain about the food, and much of this is what we call flavour. Our eyes see the food and our nose smells the food before we put it in our mouth, and already we have a conscious impression of the food in our mind; as we start to chew it our tongue and the inside of our mouth give us information about its taste, texture, warmth and spiciness. Taste is a specific sensation provided through the tongue and the back of the mouth, but the other three sensations are all aspects of touch. Indeed, the same receptor cells connecting to our brain are used to tell us if the food is hot in temperature or if it is hot meaning spicy. Finally, during chewing and swallowing, many hundreds of volatile flavour molecules pass in our breath to our olfactory organ, which is situated high inside our nose almost at the back of the eyes; this is what provides information to the brain about the odour of the food. The simple word 'flavour' is in fact a description we use to summarize the total experience we obtain from taste, touch and odour receptors during the eating of the food, and our mouth, tongue and nose are all involved in this process. It is not surprising that flavour is perhaps the most important characteristic we use in deciding whether we like our food or not and whether we will eat it again, but the question increasingly being asked is: How does this complex set of sensations work and how do we learn which flavours we like?

From research carried out in recent years it is becoming increasingly clear that our individual senses are not taken in isolation within our brain and are not processed as separate pieces of information; in fact our brain uses all the information available to it and from this creates our conscious impression of the world around us, including whatever it is we might be eating or drinking at the time. The impression we experience is certainly also influenced by information the brain has but which we may not be conscious of; for example if our body is becoming dehydrated our appreciation of a drink will be heightened. Conversely, if we have eaten a good meal and our physiological state is improved then the brain will know this and be able to relate it to the meal just eaten. If we have overeaten to the point of satiety then the brain is aware of this too, and will literally make us feel sick at the sight of more food. Trying foods and learning which ones are good is an essential part of growing up and developing from being a baby dependent on food supplied as milk from its mother to a mature adult able to survive on the food available. This is true of all mammals but is especially true for the omnivores, because they must select from a wider range of possibilities than those with more specialized diets. When we eat a food for the first time, we experience the set of sensations we call flavour and our brains relate this to our state of well-being or satisfaction after eating the food. If we eat a food and have a bad experience such as stomach-ache or nausea afterwards, the memory of that flavour will stop us eating that food for a long time afterwards, perhaps for ever. So the remembering of flavours is an important survival mechanism which we have evolved along with other animals. Human beings, however, have a unique advantage which is also a challenge: we are the only animals which do not just eat the food we can find or catch, because we have learned over many hundreds of millennia how to blend, cook and process the raw foods available to us. The fact that we could do this gave us an enormous advantage over other animals, in that we were able to survive in virtually every part of the world and on a much wider variety of food resources; through cooking and fermentation we were also able to make many foods edible which would otherwise have been poisonous and many foods storable which would have been perishable. Of course we have developed different ways of cooking and preparing foods in our many diverse cultures, and each of these has characteristic flavours which have to be learned by every new baby born into that society. What as adults we like or dislike about foods is essentially a learned response which starts at a very early age, yet it is remarkable that there is little real appreciation of this fact by parents.

It seems almost certain that we start to gain experience of flavours even from before the time we are born. Flavours from the foods that the mother eats cross the placenta and are also experienced by the unborn child, so even at this stage the learning process starts. Once the child is born, and particularly if it is fed on breast milk, it will again indirectly experience the flavours of the food eaten by the mother. Experiments carried out at the Monell Chemical Senses Laboratory in Philadelphia have shown that breast-fed babies increase their sucking rate when the mother eats either garlic or vanilla; clearly the novelty of the change in flavour is a positive experience for them. There has been considerable work done by psychologists into the development of the flavour memory of foods, and in particular why some foods are viewed with pleasure and some generate disgust. We all have our prejudices about certain foods, and foods eaten in some cultures can be considered utterly unacceptable by others. Most Europeans find the idea of eating fried insects quite disagreeable, although they are eaten in Mexico, yet the same people have no problem about eating prawns. Even population groups of similar ethnic origin can develop quite different appreciations of certain foods or flavours; it is striking that most Americans like the flavour of wintergreen whereas most Europeans find the flavour medicinal and unacceptable in food. Up until the age of about one year babies will try most foods – this doesn't mean that they will always eat them but they will try them. After the age of one year they become increasingly distrustful of anything new, and anyone who has raised children will have experienced the impossibility of getting youngsters to try new foods, particularly those that they don't like the look of, even under threat. Indeed the work of food psychologists now shows that threatening or bribing children to try a new food will simply reinforce their dislike of the idea. We learn to like foods if eating them is reinforced with a positive experience and this has to happen over a number of eating experiences. The simplest positive experience is the alleviation of hunger, and this is probably the main reinforcement process in the newborn; as the child develops, the praise of the mother or the enjoyment of the meal occasion play a part in this process. It is for this reason that the family meal is so important in developing the enjoyment of traditional family foods. Children who do not experience a wide variety of foods in positive situations at an early age will tend to have a limited acceptance of foods as they grow older, and it is largely the flavour experiences, the combinations of taste, odour and mouthfeel, which are remembered.

What seems to me remarkable is that although we encourage our children to draw, paint, play musical instruments and learn language we do little to encourage or to consciously develop their appreciation of food and flavour. Just as some individuals have an inborn talent for music or art, which in rare cases manifests itself to the level of genius, it is no doubt the case that some individuals will be more interested in food than others and some will be exceptionally talented and creative when they cook. A child with talent will always benefit from the encouragement of their innate skills; it would be remarkable if children with a liking for food and an ability to cook did not benefit from encouragement at an early age. In France they seem to have realized this, and for the last ten years the school system has introduced 'La semaine du goût' into their curriculum. The real issue, however, is that the learning of flavour is not something that can depend on one week a year; it has to happen on a daily basis and the logical place for this is around the family dining table.

Conversion Tables

All of the recipes in this book are given in metric. However, the old imperial measurements are given here, as many people still like to use this system.

An American measuring system is also given, as I don't want to exclude Americans living in this country!

These conversions are approximate and are rounded to the nearest convenient number.

Temperature

30°C	85°F	110°C	225°F	Gas 1/4	very cool
40°C	105°F	130°C	250°F	Gas 1/2	very cool
50°C	120°F	140°C	275°F	Gas 1	cool
60°C	140°F	150°C	300°F	Gas 2	slow
70°C	160°F	170°C	325°F	Gas 3	moderately slow
80°C	175°F	180°C	350°F	Gas 4	moderate
90°C	195°F	190°C	375°F	Gas 5	moderately hot
100°C	212°F	200°C	400°F	Gas 6	hot
		220°C	425°F	Gas 7	very hot
		230°C	450°F	Gas 8	very hot

Weights

10g	1/2oz	100g	3oz	300g	10oz
20g	3/4oz	150g	5oz	400g	14oz
25g	1oz	200g	6oz	450g	1lb
50g	2oz	250g	9oz	500g	1lb 2oz

Measurement of Volume

Millilitres	Fluid ounces	US	Millilitres	Fluid ounces	US	Imperial
5ml		1 teaspoon	130ml	4.5fl oz		
10ml		1 dessertspoon	140ml	5fl oz		1/4 pint
15ml	0.5fl oz	1 tablespoon	155ml	5.5fl oz	2/3 cup	
20ml			170ml	6fl oz		
25ml		5 teaspoons	185ml	6.5fl oz		
30ml	1fl oz		200ml	7fl oz		
40ml	1.5fl oz		225ml	8fl oz		
50ml		1/5 cup	255ml	9fl oz		
55ml	2fl oz		285ml	10fl oz	1 cup	1/2 pint
60ml			400ml	14fl oz		
70ml	2.5fl oz		425ml	15fl oz		3/4 pint
80ml			565ml	20fl oz	2 cup	1 pint
90ml	3.5fl oz		710ml	25fl oz		1 1/4 pints
100ml		2/5 cup	850ml	30fl oz		1 1/2 pints
115ml	4fl oz		1000ml/ 1 litre	35fl oz		1 3/4 pints

Measurement of Distance

Metric	Imperial	Metric	Imperial
5mm	$1/2$in	100mm	4in
10mm	$2/5$in	200mm	$7^3/4$in
25mm	1in	500mm	1ft $7^1/2$in
50mm	2in	1000mm/1m	3ft $3^1/2$in

Measurement of dry goods by volume, rather than weight

In many American households it is common to use volume, rather than weight, to measure out dry goods. Since the volume of a given weight of different substances (sugar, flour, etc.) depends on the density of the substance, the conversion between weight and volume depends on what is being measured. The tables below provide a range of examples for most food stuffs.

Butter, Shortening, Cheese and other Solid Fats

1 tablespoon	$1/8$ stick	$1/2$oz	15g
2 tablespoons	$1/4$ stick	1oz	30g
4 tablespoons ($1/4$ cup)	$1/2$ stick	2oz	60g
8 tablespoons ($1/2$ cup)	1 stick	4oz ($1/4$lb)	115g
16 tablespoons (1 cup)	2 sticks	8oz ($1/2$lb)	225g
32 tablespoons (2 cups)	4 sticks	16oz (1lb)	450g (500g = 0.5kg)
50g	$3^1/3$ tablespoons		
100g	$1/2$ cup minus 1 tablespoon		

Flours (unsifted)

1 tablespoon	$^{1}/_{4}$oz	8.75g
$^{1}/_{4}$ cup (4 tablespoons)	$1^{1}/_{4}$oz	35g
$^{1}/_{3}$ cup (5 tablespoons)	$1^{1}/_{2}$oz	45g
$^{1}/_{2}$ cup	$2^{1}/_{2}$oz	70g
$^{2}/_{3}$ cup	$3^{1}/_{4}$oz	90g
$^{3}/_{4}$ cup	$3^{1}/_{2}$oz	105g
1 cup	5oz	140g
$1^{1}/_{2}$ cups	$7^{1}/_{2}$oz	210g
2 cups	10oz	280g
$3^{1}/_{2}$ cups	16oz (1lb)	490g
100g	$^{3}/_{4}$ cup minus $^{1}/_{2}$ tablespoon	
250g	2 cups minus 3 tablespoons	
400g	3 cups minus 2 tablespoons	
500g	$3^{1}/_{2}$ cups minus 1 tablespoon	

Granulated Sugar

1 teaspoon	$^{1}/_{6}$oz	5g
1 tablespoon	$^{1}/_{2}$oz	15g
$^{1}/_{4}$ cup (4 tablespoons)	$1^{3}/_{4}$oz	60g
$^{1}/_{3}$ cup (5 tablespoons)	$2^{1}/_{4}$oz	75g
$^{1}/_{2}$ cup	$3^{1}/_{2}$oz	100g
$^{2}/_{3}$ cup	$4^{1}/_{2}$oz	130g
$^{3}/_{4}$ cup	5oz	150g
1 cup	7oz	200g
$1^{1}/_{2}$ cups	$9^{1}/_{2}$oz	300g
2 cups	$13^{1}/_{2}$oz	400g
100g	$^{1}/_{2}$ cup	
250g	1 cup plus 3 tablespoons plus 1 teaspoon	
400g	2 cups	
500g	$2^{1}/_{2}$ cups	

Other equivalents

Breadcrumbs

Dry	3/4 cup	4oz	115g
Fresh	2 cups	4oz	115g
Brown sugar	1 1/2 cups	1lb	450g
Confectioners' sugar	4 cups	1lb	450g

Egg whites

1	2 tablespoons		
8	1 cup		

Egg yolks

1	1 tablespoon		
16	1 cup		

Fruit, dried and pitted

Plumped	2 2/3 cups	1lb	450g
Cooked and puréed	2 1/3 cups	1lb	450g

Fruits, fresh, such as apples

Raw and sliced	3 cups	1lb	450g
Cooked and chopped	1 1/3 cups	1lb	450g
Puréed	1 1/4 cups	1lb	450g

Nuts

Chopped	3/4 cup	4oz	115g
Ground	1 cup, loosely packed	4oz	115g

Vegetables

Carrots and other roots

Sliced	3 cups	1lb	450g
Puréed	1 1/3 cups	1lb	450g
Onions, sliced or chopped	3 cups	1lb	450g
Potatoes, raw, sliced or chopped	3 cups	1lb	450g
Spinach and other leafy greens	1 1/2 cups	1lb	450g

Liquid and Dry Measure Equivalents (US)

		Liquid	Dry
2 tablespoons	1oz	25ml	30g
1 cup	¼ quart	250ml	225g
2 cups	1 pint	500ml	450g
4 cups	32oz	1000ml/1 litre	
4 quarts	1 gallon	3.75 litres	

Ounces to grams	multiply by 28.35
Teaspoons to millilitres	multiply by 5
Tablespoons to millilitres	multiply by 15
Fluid ounces to millilitres	multiply by 30
Cups to litres	multiply by 0.24
Fahrenheit to Celsius	subtract 32, multiply by 5, divide by 9

Snacks

How often as an adult have you wanted to eat something outside of mealtimes and, having sifted through the fridge and cupboards, ended up eating some form of junk, processed or additive-laden food? This is an area of eating which is really useful for introducing children to new ingredients and flavours. They will be far more excited and eager to indulge in food if they have been involved in cooking it and know what the ingredients are.

How fantastic would it be for them to snack on home-made baked beans with real tomato ketchup made from fresh tomatoes? To discover the tastes and smells of proper cheeses by savouring cheese on toast made not from grilling mass-produced Cheddar on a slice of toasted bread, but by gently baking the bread and cheese in the oven?

Many of these snacks can be made in quantity so that they can be ready in the time it takes to open a can and toast a piece of bread. Even homemade biscuits are relatively simple, and although they contain butter and sugar they are far more beneficial than the mass-produced, additive-laden alternatives available in the shops.

Any kitchen task a child can perform will help to break down the mystique of food and eating, making it accessible and enjoyable. A child with few eating hang-ups will be a child with greater self-confidence, able to enjoy fully one of life's greatest pleasures – the joy of the table and the social inter-action which accompanies it.

Tomato Ketchup

In seventeenth-century England ketchup was a condiment, pickled and fermented using a base of mushrooms or walnuts with acidic grape juice, but the name now seems to apply only to tomatoes. There are numerous variations on this popular household food product, and, without wanting to appear to be a walking advert for Heinz, their ketchup is about the best on the market. However, it's possible to make a homemade version using fresh ingredients. This recipe can be fiddled around with, depending on your children's tastes and also, to a certain extent, on what you have in your kitchen. Use the best tomatoes that you can afford.

★ **Children's tip**
Let your child grind up the different spices to make four-spice. Put equal quantities of allspice, cloves, mace and cinnamon into a pestle and mortar and crush until finely ground.

Core and halve the tomatoes, then roughly chop them and put them into a casserole. Cover with a cartouche and bring to the boil, then simmer for 10 minutes.

★ **Tip**
A cartouche is basically a paper lid that partially covers the top of the braising liquid in a pan. It enables some of the steam to be retained and helps to cook the parts of the food that are not immersed in the

liquid. These 'lids' are used frequently in commercial kitchens and, as you will see later on in the book, are essential when poaching fruits.

All you need to do to make one is to take a square of parchment paper and fold it in half twice, turning the paper 90° between each fold. Now fold this square in half diagonally so that you have a triangular piece of paper. Hold it over the pan that you will be using so that the point of the triangle is in the centre of the pan, and tear or cut off the end in line with the rim in a slight curve. Open out the paper and you should be left with a roughly circular piece of paper that is about the same size as the pan.

All you need to do now is to pierce the paper with a knife half a dozen times or so. This means that when you put the cartouche on top of the liquid and press down lightly, you will force some of the liquid through the holes to sit on top of the paper during cooking. The paper will both cover the liquid, keeping any ingredients being poached or braised from protruding too much, and will also allow steam to escape.

Our children always make these for us now!

Makes approximately 500ml

5kg very ripe best-quality tomatoes

200g onions, chopped

4 cloves of confit garlic (see page 196) or 2 cloves of garlic

1 tablespoon Dijon mustard

1 tablespoon white wine vinegar

8 cloves

2 coffeespoons salt

1 teaspoon four-spice or Chinese five-spice

a good pinch of ground ginger

a pinch of cayenne pepper (make sure you don't overdo this)

6¹/₂ soupspoons icing sugar

Pass the tomatoes through a fine-meshed sieve into another casserole, and add all the other ingredients except the icing sugar. Simmer until the mixture is reduced by approximately half and begins to thicken.

Push the mixture through a fine-meshed sieve again, return it to the casserole, and add the icing sugar. Put the casserole back on to the heat. Whisking regularly so that the ketchup does not catch and burn, bring to a simmer and cook until the desired thickness and flavour are achieved.

Pour the mixture into a sterilized preserving jar, seal, and stand the jar in simmering water for 40 minutes. The ketchup will then keep for several months.

★ **Children's tip**

This is a good recipe for children to get involved in: it shows them that it is possible to make from natural ingredients something which, to them, only exists as a product in a bottle. It may also serve to introduce children who like ketchup but not tomatoes to this fruit in other shapes or forms.

Although this recipe may seem lengthy, it is fairly straightforward – children aged eight upwards could, if supervised, make it themselves. Imagine your son or daughter being able to make their own tomato ketchup!

The following three vegetable dishes have many uses. They are great in sandwiches, with cheese or any type of ham or chorizo; on toasted bread or baguettes, also called 'tartines' in France; mixed with pasta; served with fried or scrambled eggs as a light meal or even as a garnish for a main meal.

Red Peppers Marinated with Anchovies

For this recipe you need marinated anchovies, not the tinned, salted ones – they are too strong.

3 red peppers

200ml extra virgin olive oil, plus a little to brush the peppers

75g marinated anchovies

2 cloves of garlic

1 bunch of fresh thyme

25ml sherry vinegar

salt and freshly ground black pepper

Preheat the grill. Core and halve the red peppers and remove all the white pith and seeds (see Gazpacho, page 121). Put the pepper halves skin side up on a grill tray and brush or rub them all over with olive oil. Don't worry if the oil runs off on to the tray – it will be used for marinating. Put the peppers under the grill and – this is very important – leave them there until they are charred. They need to be black all over. They will not taste burnt but will have a wonderful smoked flavour.

While the peppers are grilling, finely chop the anchovies, reserving any oil, and bash each garlic clove.

Reserve a couple of sprigs of thyme for garnishing and tie the rest up into a bundle.

Heat the olive oil in a frying pan over a medium heat, add the anchovies, garlic and thyme, and cook for 5 minutes. Pour in the vinegar and bring to the boil, then remove from the heat, season with salt and pepper, and leave to cool.

Remove the blackened peppers from the grill. While they are still hot, put them into a freezer bag and seal, or wrap them in clingfilm. Leave them to cool for 10 minutes, after which time you should be able to peel them easily, but hold them under cold running water if not. Cut the peppers into slices and combine them with the anchovy mixture, reserved anchovy oil and any juices from the grill tray. Leave for several hours or overnight.

Strain some or all of the oil off before serving.

Some chopped fresh basil or picked thyme leaves would work really well in this dish.

★ Children's tip

Thyme leaves make a wonderful garnish to many dishes. You will probably be thinking that life is too short to pick thyme leaves, but the kids will happily oblige and it really does make a difference.

Compote of Onions and Sage

Peel the onions and slice them as finely as possible. Put them into a pan with half the butter. Add 10 of the sage leaves to the pan. Cover the onions and sage with a cartouche (see page 50). Put the pan on to a high heat, and when the butter is bubbling, turn the heat right down to a simmer. Now you can either leave the pan on a low heat on the burner, or put it in the oven preheated to 110°C/gas mark 1/4. The onions need to be cooked for at least 2 hours, preferably longer, until they are completely soft and broken down. It is important to check every now and then that they are not getting too hot or they will 'catch' and become bitter. Add a little water if necessary.

4 onions
150g unsalted butter
20 fresh sage leaves
a few drops of sherry vinegar or balsamic vinegar

Half-way through the cooking time, heat the remaining butter with the rest of the sage leaves until the butter turns a light golden brown and the leaves just begin to sizzle. Leave to cool down, then pour the butter through a strainer directly on to the onions. Stir, and continue cooking. When done, these onions should be soft and fragrantly sweet, golden but not caramelized.

Finally, add the vinegar to taste – just enough to balance the sweetness.

★ Children's tip

Let your children pile the sage leaves on top of each other and roll them backwards and forwards with the palm of their hand on the work surface. They will be amazed how aromatic the leaves become when this is done. It releases a lot of the natural oils and brings out the flavour of the sage.

Confit Tomatoes

It is a sad state of affairs that some of the most expensive tomatoes to be found in our supermarkets are marketed as having been grown 'especially for flavour'. Why else should one ever want to buy a tomato?

Unfortunately we have forgotten what many foods should taste of, and with the fierce price wars that are developing in the supermarkets the situation could become worse. People will come to expect many of their raw ingredients to cost less and less, and this in turn will make quality ingredients seem too expensive to many people.

It is vital for our children to discover the true taste of food rather than that of the over-farmed, chemically engineered and mass-produced nonsense that is often sold as such.

This method of cooking tomatoes appears in many cookery books and in many variations, with differing results. My preference is to use an oven temperature that half cooks and half dries them. Peeling and deseeding the tomatoes helps to remove some of their acidity, so that the end result is sweeter.

Preheat the oven to 110°C/gas mark ¼.

Peel and very finely slice the garlic. Cut each basil leaf in half and break up the thyme sprigs. Roughly chop the bay leaves.

Bring a medium-sized saucepan of water to the boil. With the pointed end of a potato peeler or a small sharp knife, cut out the core of each tomato and make a very slight crossed slit

1 clove of garlic
10 fresh basil leaves
10 sprigs of fresh thyme
2 fresh bay leaves
10 tomatoes
extra virgin olive oil
salt and freshly ground black pepper
1/2 level teaspoon caster sugar

on the underside. Carefully drop the tomatoes into the boiling water for 10 seconds, then lift them out and plunge them into iced water. The skins can now be peeled off easily. If the tomatoes are not quite ripe enough they may need to be returned to the boiling water for a few seconds. Don't leave them in the water for too long or they'll become mushy.

Now slice the tomatoes in half vertically and scoop out the seeds, making sure that you remove the white pith. Dab the insides dry with kitchen paper. If you have time, leave the tomatoes on a few layers of kitchen paper for an hour or so to allow them to dry a little before the next stage.

Generously brush the tomatoes all over with the olive oil and lay them out on a baking sheet, cut sides up. Into each cavity put a slice of garlic, some basil, bay and thyme. Season lightly with salt and pepper and sprinkle with the sugar.

Cook in the preheated oven for approximately 4 hours, turning the tomatoes half-way through.

The cooking time will vary depending on the ripeness of the tomatoes. When done, they will have turned a vibrant, deep red and be slightly wrinkled. You can then put them into an airtight container, covered in olive oil and with all of the aromatics with which they were cooked. They will keep for at least a month.

These tomatoes are delicious in sandwiches, perhaps with some onion compote (see page 55), or maybe with fried eggs (see next recipe) – in fact, to be quite honest, they're delicious with just about anything! The oil that they are preserved in works well in a vinaigrette or as a dressing for cooked pasta.

★ Children's tip

Here is an interesting taste experiment to try with your children. Take 2 confit tomatoes and sprinkle one of them lightly with caster sugar. Without making any comment, watch their reaction! As adults most of us are so preconditioned to what we eat that we have a sort of automatic barrier against foods that we are not used to – whether it be unfamiliar ingredients or, as in this case, the idea of eating a tomato as a sweet. If you think about it, though, tomatoes are a fruit (like anything else with seeds on the inside). And tomato jam is not that unusual!

Fried Egg

Why a recipe for fried egg? Well, eggs are a healthy source of protein and very beneficial for children. They also make a great snack, on toast or as a light dinner with homemade baked beans (see page 73). The main reason for including this particular recipe, however, is the simple but clever method of obtaining a perfectly cooked yolk and white. Normally, if you get a nice, gently cooked white you will be left with a cold floppy yolk, and if you want a perfect yolk, the white will be tough and overcooked.

This recipe comes from Bernard Loiseau, whose eponymous restaurant in Burgundy has three Michelin stars.

Ideally, you will need a stainless steel egg ring and a small non-stick frying pan. The egg ring is not essential, it just helps to hold the shape of the white. It is very important to use fresh eggs for this, so that the white will remain compact and not run everywhere.

Obviously eggs keep better in the fridge; however, they should be at room temperature before you cook them – the main reason for boiled eggs cracking is the drastic change of temperature caused by using them straight from the fridge. If you do keep your eggs in the fridge, just put them into a bowl of hot, not boiling, water for a couple of minutes at the most before using them.

For those of you who don't know how to tell whether or not an egg is fresh, here are two methods that will help:

1. A fresh egg put into a bowl of water at least 15cm deep will immediately sink to the bottom. This is because the pocket of air contained in one end of the egg will be tiny. In an egg that is 1 week old, this air pocket will have expanded and will cause the egg to begin to float, with the more rounded air-filled end nearer the surface. After this egg has reached 2–3 weeks old it will float vertically, as the air in the rounded end has expanded that much.

2. Simply crack the egg: the white in a fresh egg will remain compact around the yolk. An egg that is less than fresh will demonstrate the fact by having a white that is semi-liquid.

Egg shells have become a lot more fragile, over the years, as you may have noticed. This is because through continually breeding chickens in order to get the most yielding egg, the contents of the egg itself have increased without the shell becoming any thicker. Subsequently, the shell has had to stretch to cover the increased volume that it has to hold. This has meant a thinner and therefore more delicate shell.

1 best-quality free-range egg
a knob of butter
a few drops of balsamic vinegar
salt and freshly ground black pepper

Preheat the oven to 250°C/gas mark 9.

Break the egg and carefully separate the white from the yolk, making sure you keep the yolk whole.

Put the butter into the frying pan with a soupspoon of water and heat until foaming (the water just helps to stop the butter from getting too hot, which would cause the egg white to brown and toughen). When the butter is beginning to foam, carefully slide in the white.

Put the pan into the preheated oven and cook the white for 1½ minutes. The top should still be trembling. Put the raw yolk into the centre of the white and return the pan to the oven for 2 minutes.

Sprinkle a few drops of balsamic vinegar on to the egg, season, and serve.

You can, if this feels like too much hassle, cook fried eggs in the usual way. Just remember the following points:

- Use the best unsalted butter or oil possible.
- Do not have the pan too hot or too cold: too hot and the white of the egg will be overdone before the rest has time to cook, too cold and the egg white will begin to run.
- Cover the pan: this way you will obtain a more even cooking; be careful, as the egg will cook quicker.
- Only ever salt the egg at the last minute – just before you are about to eat it will be ideal.

★ Children's tip
A few words about eggs, chickens and children! It's very important for children to gain a full understanding of animal welfare and farming; they will then be in a position to make their own decisions about the quality and nature of what they eat. Chickens and eggs are a good example of this! The battery chicken is no longer an animal but an egg-producing machine. One of my first jobs was on the local chicken farm, egg-collecting. I can remember at the time being dwarfed in a barn that seemed the size of a ship, with cages that seemed to tower to the roof. I spent five hours on a Saturday and Sunday morning collecting over 2,000 eggs in a feathery haze. For a generous £3 a day, it was character-building!

Chickens are known as indiscriminate layers, in that if a hen is due to lay a total of ten eggs and two are removed before she has finished, she will think that she has still two eggs to lay. A free-range hen will also lay more eggs during the warmer months, and to replicate these conditions, battery hens are kept under artificial light. As if all of this isn't enough, the hens are crammed into a cage so that they have no room to move and therefore no energy is wasted on anything other than laying. This cramped lifestyle breeds disease, thus requiring the hens to be pumped full of antibiotics.

All of this might sound depressing in itself, but it also has a significant detrimental effect on the nutritional and flavour qualities in the egg itself. It is quite interesting that some moral vegetarians will still buy battery eggs!

The good news is that free-range eggs not only taste better, they are more nutritious and come from happy birds.

Cheese on Toast

This is a blueprint for numerous variations, depending on your tastes and those of your child. It presents a fantastic opportunity to experiment and involve your children. As with many of these recipes, it is very important to understand that they are not cast in stone.

The first, obvious point of variation is the cheese. You can use almost any type, and while it will probably make sense to begin with Cheddar, as the most recognizable-tasting cheese, it is a great way of introducing kids to the whole range of cheeses: the Swiss cheeses such as Gruyère and Emmenthal, goat's cheese, blue cheeses, Bries, etc.

The bread can be brushed or spread with butter or olive oil and rubbed with garlic. If you have made any confit garlic (see page 196), this would be delicious spread on the bread.

You can also put various ingredients under the cheese to give extra flavour: marinated peppers (see page 53), onion compote (see page 55), pissaladière (see page 271) or confit tomatoes (see page 57).

Toasting buttered bread in the oven gives you a lovely delicate crust with a moist centre.

Preheat the oven to 250°C/gas mark 9.

Spread thick slices of good-quality bread with butter or olive oil. You could use a baguette sliced in half lengthways. Cut a clove of garlic in half and rub the cut face of the garlic over the bread. It's up to you how much you rub on and also how hard you rub, depending on how garlicky you want your bread to taste. Lay the bread on a baking sheet, put into the preheated oven, and bake for up to 5 minutes.

Top the bread with onion compote, marinated peppers, or other such garnish, then with thinly sliced cheese. Drizzle with white wine. (The wine is not essential; it is really up to you.) Return the bread to the oven and cook until the cheese is melted, bubbling and delicious.

★ Variation
If you decide to make this regularly, you could make some garlic wine and either keep it for this recipe or use it to replace white wine generally in the kitchen. Bring a bottle of white wine to the boil with 10 crushed cloves of garlic and some fresh herbs (thyme, rosemary and tarragon, for example). Add a coffeespoon of crushed peppercorns. Boil for a couple of minutes, then remove from the heat and leave to cool. Pour into an airtight container and strain before using.

Open Toasted Sandwiches

These are a great base for snacks, as the variations are almost endless. You can even make a dessert version, as you will see.

If you use a baguette sliced in half, you have several choices of spread:

- Butter, salted or unsalted.
- Olive oil: you can half freeze extra virgin oil and use it as a spread.
- Animal fat such as beef, pork or lamb, very old-fashioned but perhaps not the most healthy choice these days.
- Duck fat, which can either be purchased from some supermarkets or delicatessens or collected from a roast duck. The good news here is that duck fat has noticeably less cholesterol than butter and has many uses.

The bread itself can be toasted, but as in the previous recipe you will be well rewarded by spreading the bread and then grilling or roasting it until done.

Here are some examples for toppings.

Scrambled Egg and Chorizo Topping

Chorizo is a cured pork and paprika sausage that can be bought raw or cooked from most supermarkets. When chorizo is cooked it leaks delicious orange-tinged oil, which is fantastic with most things. Here, it is combined with scrambled egg.

When scrambling eggs, simply place them in the pan on a very low heat and stir continually. The mix will begin to thicken and will become grainy, almost like the texture of instant porridge. This will take 10–15 minutes. The important thing is to be patient and keep the heat as low as possible.

You will find that, at the right level, the eggs will not thicken much at all for at least 10 minutes; they may take a little more than 15 minutes to cook, depending on how many eggs you are scrambling. You will find it easier to use a whisk than a spoon, as it keeps the egg moving so that it will not catch. Remove from the heat while the mix is still a little runny, as the residual heat will still continue to cook the eggs.

Slice the chorizo and grill until cooked. Reserve the oil.

Lightly beat a few eggs with a generous amount of salt and freshly ground black pepper and put into a pan on a low heat with a knob or two of butter. Be patient. To give you some idea of the ideal temperature, it should take at least 10 minutes to reach the consistency of very slightly grainy thick custard. Be patient; trust me!

Finish the cooking with a teaspoon of crème fraîche or

cream, and add a knob of cold butter; then stir in the oil from the chorizo.

Lay some of the cooked chorizo slices on the toasted bread. Spoon the eggs on top and serve.

Sardine, Mackerel, Smoked Salmon or Tuna Topping

Blend tinned fish or smoked salmon with softened butter and a touch of crushed garlic. Even better, add a little garlic wine (see page 65) if you have any and/or some confit garlic (see page 196). Use approximately 50g of butter for every 125g of fish, a little less if using smoked salmon.

Season with salt and freshly ground black pepper if necessary, and add cayenne pepper to taste. You could also add some lemon juice or a few drops of Worcestershire sauce.

Spread a thin layer of onion compote (see page 55) on the bread, place the fish on top of that, and serve.

Dessert Toasts

Here are a couple of suggestions.

You can use confit tomatoes (4 per person, see page 57), or fresh tomatoes (2–3 per person), skinned, deseeded and chopped.

Put 2 knobs of unsalted butter in a frying pan over a medium heat. When it is sizzling add ½ teaspoon of icing sugar per person if using confit tomatoes and 1 heaped teaspoon if using fresh tomatoes. When this starts to brown, add the tomatoes and grill for a minute or two.

Put the tomatoes on to the toast. Reduce the tomato juice, adding some vanilla seeds or extract if you like, and pour over the tomatoes.

Spoon a little cream on top and serve.

Take some strawberries, remove the stems and lightly crush the berries with a fork, adding a little unrefined caster sugar to taste. Spread them on the toast.

You can add freshly ground black pepper, lemon juice or even a little extra virgin olive oil to the strawberry mixture. Instead of bread you could use a slice of brioche, or ciabatta if using olive oil.

★ Tip

When we eat certain foods, the brain can effectively heighten the flavour by association. An example is sugar with banana flavour.

Professor Andy Taylor from Nottingham University ran a test on me a few months ago. He fed me a sugar solution and a banana flavour at the same time through a tube. I had to turn an indicator switch up and down with my perception of the intensity of the banana flavour.

With the banana and the syrup coming into my mouth at the same time, the banana flavour was pretty strong. The sugar was then turned down so that I was being fed banana flavour and water and as the sugar decreased, to my amazement, so too did the banana flavour. The sugar was then gradually introduced and as it went up, so too did the banana flavour – incredible! All the time the banana flavour was still being fed to me at the same rate, only the concentration of sugar was changing.

Then the most amazing thing happened when the banana flavour was turned off and the syrup was still being fed through. I still perceived banana!

This amazing result really just demonstrates that our memory of flavour behaves in the same way as our memory of anything else. If we see a car, for example, we may remember the make or colour of the car or even the colour of the number plate. We are far less likely to remember how many people were in that car or if it had a scratch on the side of it. Our memory will try not to work overtime unless it has to.

With flavours, the same thing happens. As we grow up on a sugar-based diet, our memory will latch on to the sugar more than the banana flavour. When the sugar level is adjusted, our perception of flavour adjusts with it. If I were to be fed the banana flavour first, this experiment would be nowhere near as effective. It was the fact that the sugar and banana were fed to me at the same time that caused my flavour memory to track the sugar more than the banana.

★ Children's tip

Here's a little experiment you can conduct with your children. Crush some strawberries with sugar and some without. Don't let them know which is which, just let them taste and guess for themselves. Obviously it is important not to put too much or too little sugar with the strawberries.

Apple Toasts

Preheat the oven to 190°C/gas mark 5.

Peel, halve and core the apples. Quarter them and put them into a casserole with 40g of the butter, 40g of the sugar and the cinnamon stick. Cover and cook in the oven for 40 minutes, then remove the cinnamon stick and, if necessary, bring the contents of the casserole to the boil to reduce any juices that may remain.

Serves 4

500g Braeburn or Cox apples
70g unsalted butter
60g unrefined caster sugar
1 cinnamon stick
100ml double cream
4 nice slices of bread

Lightly whip the cream.

Toast the slices of bread; butter them with the rest of the butter, adding a little more if necessary. Top with the apple compote. Finally spoon a little whipped cream on top, sprinkle with the remaining sugar and put under the grill until the sugar is beginning to brown.

To give an extra dimension, grate a little raw apple on top of the finished dish and taste the difference! As always, make sure that you and your children taste before and after so that the difference is really noticeable.

Baked Beans

This recipe is here for much the same reason as the tomato ketchup one on page 50. By giving children an understanding of a food many of them consume passionately and that they think can only ever come out of a tin, the door to the possibilities of cooking can be opened.

The method may seem a little long but the tomato fondue can be made in advance and kept in the fridge in an airtight container. It will keep for several weeks.

Before you start, a few words about dried beans. One of the more difficult and infuriating processes in the kitchen is cooking dried beans properly. They either end up hard like bullets, or break up before they are cooked properly. We have done quite a bit of work on this subject at the restaurant with my friend Peter Barham of Bristol University. Peter has written a very good book on the science of cooking, one that is approachable by all domestic cooks.

It seems as if every cookery book contains conflicting advice on how to cook dried beans. Some will tell you that it is necessary to break down or soften the outer skin of the bean to allow the cooking liquid to penetrate the interior without splitting the bean. One thing, however, is for sure. If the outer skin is blemished or cracked when raw, the bean will split during cooking. You must, therefore, buy the best-quality pulses you can, and just have a quick glance through the packet to make sure that there are as few cracks as possible. The quality of the pulse depends on how and when they were dried. The fresher the better. Many cookery books will tell you to pre-soak the beans. This is supposedly to prepare the outside of the beans so that they will soften more readily during the initial boiling stage. Some recipes will tell you to soak the beans overnight, others say 2 hours is sufficient.

The initial pre-boiling stage is to soften the skins so that they allow the cooking medium to penetrate the bean while still holding it together.

Many books will tell you not to salt the beans until near the end of the cooking process. Others will tell you not to cook them in an acid environment, for example, with tomatoes, as they will not cook properly.

Last night I decided that the best way to test these theories was to cook some beans, doing several things that I should apparently not do! I took some temperamental dried haricot beans and, without pre-soaking them, put them into a stone oven dish. I blended some tomato fondue with water and poured this over the beans. Next, I added aromatics and generously seasoned the mix.

I covered the pot and put it into the oven at 110°C/gas mark ¼. After some 3 hours, the beans were still not cooked. As it was now very late, three o'clock in the morning, I had to go to bed! Disappointed, I turned the oven off and retired slightly hurt.

This morning I tried the beans and was amazed; they were soft inside, with the skins nicely broken down but still completely intact. So I have reproduced the recipe here.

As with green vegetables, calcium or hard water is an enemy of pulses. If you have hard water, cooking the beans in distilled water, which you can buy from petrol stations sold as battery water, would do the trick! Failing this, Volvic mineral water is very neutral and relatively low in calcium.

If you ever have the opportunity to buy fresh haricot beans, usually sold as coco or borlotti beans, do try them – they are fantastic. They will need nothing other than podding and cooking.

★ **Tip**

The tomato fondue can be made in a large batch, as it keeps brilliantly. You might as well make extra, especially if you have extra little hands to help you to peel and deseed the tomatoes! It can be used for many different things: finishing risottos, mixing with pasta, spread on toast, perhaps with an egg or even as a garnish with some fish or sausages.

Sweat the onion in the olive oil with the spices for 10 minutes on a very low heat. Add the garlic and the bouquet garni and continue to sweat for another 5 minutes. Add the tomatoes, tomato juices, Tabasco and Worcestershire sauce, ketchup and vinegar, then add the lemon zest and cook on a very low heat for 3–4 hours, adding the saffron, if using, 45 minutes into the cooking time.

When cooked, the fondue should be dark red and almost jam-like. Don't worry if any oil has split out of the mix, it can just be poured off. In fact this oil will be delicious and can be used in many dishes.

For the tomato fondue

1 onion, peeled and very finely chopped

125ml extra virgin olive oil

1/2 star anise

2 cloves

1 heaped teaspoon coriander seeds

2 cloves of garlic, peeled and minced

a bouquet garni consisting of thyme, celery leaf, parsley and bay leaf tied with a strip of leek

650g best-quality tomatoes, skinned, deseeded and chopped, the juices strained and reserved

a few drops of Tabasco

a few drops of Worcestershire sauce

1 dessertspoon of tomato ketchup, home-made if you have it (see page 50)

25ml best-quality sherry vinegar

finely grated lemon zest to taste

10 strands of saffron (optional)

Preheat the oven to 110°C/gas mark ¼.

Purée the tomato fondue in a blender with a little of the oil from the fondue or, failing that, olive oil, and a touch of water if necessary. There should be enough purée to cover the beans by 1–2cm.

Put the beans into an ovenproof dish. Cover with the tomato purée and add all the other ingredients. Season generously.

Cover the dish, using tin foil if you have no lid, and place it in the oven. After 3 hours, turn off the oven and leave the beans to cool down.

Simple as that!

★ Tip

Contrary to what many recipes say, salt can be added at the beginning of the cooking process without toughening the beans up. It may slow down the cooking time, but with a long gentle braise there is no problem at all. After all, how many recipes for cooking pulses advise salting only towards the end but have no problem in telling you to add a large slab of salty smoked bacon to the pot at the beginning!

For the beans

tomato fondue (see page 75)

extra virgin olive oil

200g dried haricot beans (the best quality available)

1 onion, peeled and halved, studded with 2 cloves

3 carrots, topped, tailed and halved lengthways

3 cloves of garlic, peeled

bouquet garni (thyme, rosemary, bay leaf)

1 stick of celery

1 leek, cut crossways into 3 pieces

75g unsalted butter

salt and freshly ground black pepper

You can add various flavourings depending on your taste: some smoked bacon, chorizo or sausage would work really well; just add them half-way through the cooking time. Our eldest daughter adores clams baked with the beans for half an hour.

Once made, these beans will keep for a few weeks, longer if you put them into a sterilized preserving jar.

There is another technique that works well for cooking beans – the good old-fashioned method of pressure-cooking. How many of you remember being shouted at by your mother because you ruined her stew or soup by releasing the pressure on the cooker? For a child, it was like an addiction; standing at the doorway of the kitchen and jumping up and down as much as possible until the little valve on top of the pressure-cooker popped up. The gentle, reassuring sound of pressure doing its job in the kitchen gave way to a high-pitched hiss that meant you were in big trouble!

Probably the most memorable piece of kitchen equipment from my childhood, the pressure-cooker has recently been creeping back into the Fat Duck kitchen. Under the right circumstances, cooking dried beans under pressure works wonders. A little while ago, one of my chefs was in the local gym on his afternoon break when he got chatting to someone who turned out to be a retired quality controller for Heinz. I made sure that the next time he met this chap, the chef would extract as much information as possible. At the time we were doing a lot of work on cooking dried pulses, and I wondered how tinned-bean companies managed to get the beans nicely cooked and completely un-split. The sauce they are cooked in can sometimes be very questionable but the texture of the bean itself is as it should be.

The gentleman informed us that the beans were cooked in the tin with their sauce. After discussions with Peter, we decided to try cooking the beans under pressure, in the tomato sauce, with very good results.

Cooked in a pressure-cooker, the beans take between 35 and

50 minutes. Simply put all the ingredients into the cooker, bring to the boil and cook on low heat with the pressure set to medium. After 20 minutes, release the pressure and leave to stand for 10–15 minutes before removing the lid. If the beans are not yet done, just put them back on the heat to simmer until ready.

★ **Variation**

You can, as a slight variation, reheat these beans and crush them with a fork into a purée, adding some goose fat, butter or olive oil. This is delicious on toast, and is an interesting demonstration of how by simply changing the texture you can also alter the taste. A good example of this is the way that a potato that has been mashed until smooth will taste different from one that has been crushed with a fork so that it retains texture.

There are numerous small exercises like this that you can do to show children that cooking is not a daunting, mysterious chore but an area where they can enjoy themselves and make food completely approachable, fun, and above all delicious.

Some of these recipes may seem a little lengthy for a snack, but they will keep and you will be well rewarded by the extra effort. More importantly, however, hopefully this chapter has demonstrated the variations available and encouraged you to get experimenting. Of course, one of life's great and healthy snacks requires virtually no preparation at all: fruit!

Grains

Grains are probably the most versatile and approachable food for your children. Having said that, I fondly remember trying to convince my son Jack that tagliatelle was no different from the spaghetti that he normally likes. Unfortunately, at the age of four, he did not seem to understand!

One of the great things about these dishes is that they tend to be very family-oriented – you can put a big bowl of food on the table and let everyone help themselves. Just think of the mess!

Pasta

These recipes use top-quality dried semolina pasta. Personally, with a few exceptions, I am not a fan of most of the fresh pasta that is available in supermarkets. It tends to be starchy and characterless. Top-quality dried semolina pasta is far superior. You can, of course, make your own pasta, which can be good fun and a great experience for your children. You need a pasta machine, the correct flour and a little patience, but, after a couple of attempts, it really is quite easy. You will find a basic pasta recipe on page 89 if you want to give it a go. (And if you want to cook ravioli, it is definitely better to make it yourself.)

There are some key points that should be followed when cooking pasta:

- Make sure you have a pot big enough. Too often you see people filling a small saucepan with water and trying to cram in as much pasta as possible. The trouble with this is that the amount of starch released by the pasta as it cooks is too much to be sufficiently diluted in the small amount of water, so that it becomes gluey, affecting the end result.

- Never use less than 2 litres of water, even for a small amount of pasta. Ideally, use as much water as you can keep on a rolling boil.

- Salt the pasta water. Remember the ratio 1:10:100. 1 litre water; 10g salt; 100g pasta.

- Many recipes advocate pouring some olive oil into the cooking water to stop the pasta sticking. This is pointless, as the oil simply floats to the surface, forming a small puddle. The only time when it may be beneficial is when cooking sheets of pasta. You can place these in the boiling water, ensuring that they become coated with oil as they go into the pan. If you want to stop the pasta sticking, just drain it once it is cooked and immediately coat it in olive oil.

- Always plunge the pasta into boiling salted water and stir the water with a wooden spoon. This will stop the pasta sticking from the beginning.

- The pasta is ready when it is 'al dente'. This translates to 'to the tooth', and is the stage when the pasta is cooked but still offers some resistance. Ideally, it is the moment when the chalky centre of the pasta disappears but before it becomes soft. The best way to tell is to keep tasting.

- Make sure you always have a colander at the ready – the last thing you want is to have your pasta ready, only to have to start rummaging around for the colander.

- Once the pasta is cooked, drain it by lifting it out of the water with tongs, a slotted spoon or a sieve; do not tip the whole contents of the pan out into the colander, as you will simply be pouring the starchy water back over the pasta.

- Once drained, immediately coat the pasta in olive oil, butter or any sauce that you may want to serve with it.

- If you are planning on eating the pasta with just oil and Parmesan cheese, for example, it is a good idea to use a little of the starchy cooking water to create a little sauce. This is a very traditional technique.

Carbonara

This is my version of the classic Italian pasta dish, which originally came from Marcella Hazan's fantastic book, *Essentials of Classic Italian Cooking*.

For me, the beauty of it is that unlike most carbonaras it contains no cream. Always use Parmigiano-Reggiano cheese, which is now readily available in all supermarkets, never buy pre-grated Parmesan – it's disgusting. This is our children's favourite quick dinner.

Serves 4

3 onions

2 cloves of garlic

salt and freshly ground black pepper

extra virgin olive oil

200g smoked streaky bacon, sliced into 1cm thick lardons

1 fresh green chilli, chopped, seeds and white pith removed (optional, depending on your children's taste)

400g top-quality dried semolina pasta (spaghetti would be ideal for this dish)

3 egg yolks

50g Parmesan cheese

1 bunch of fresh parsley (optional)

Peel, halve and de-root the onions and chop them finely.

Peel the garlic and purée it with the back of a chopping knife; to do this, roughly chop it and sprinkle over some salt. Now, using the flat of the knife, drag it backwards across the garlic. Repeat this action several times until you have a garlic purée.

Pour about 75ml of olive oil into a frying pan, add the onions and garlic, and cook on a low to medium heat for about 15 minutes.

Meanwhile, put the water on for the pasta; using the ratio mentioned on page 82, bring 4 litres of water to the boil, adding 40g of salt.

Try to regulate the temperature of the frying pan so that up to this point the onions have not started to colour. Add the bacon and chilli and turn up the heat. Cook the onions and bacon until they become nicely browned and the edges of the onions begin to catch.

By this time, the water should be boiling. Plunge in the pasta and cook on a gentle boil until al dente. While the pasta is boiling, put the egg yolks into a bowl that will be large enough to hold the pasta and grate the Parmesan on to the yolks.

Have a colander at the ready: drain the pasta by lifting it out of the liquid (see page 83) and into the colander. Shake the colander to drain off the liquid, and before all the cooking water has been drained off, tip the pasta on to the egg and cheese mixture. You should have about 1–2 tablespoons of cooking water still left around the pasta; this will help to form the sauce.

Immediately mix the pasta so that it is bound with the egg and cheese. Tip the contents of the frying pan on to the pasta and mix thoroughly. Season, sprinkle with chopped parsley if using, and serve.

This is a real winner!

This dish is a great blueprint and has many variations, depending on your children's tastes. You can also use it to introduce your kids to new flavours:

- Our children adore it with peas mixed in; simply add 100g of frozen peas to the frying pan with the onions and bacon and cook for 3–4 minutes. Put the peas into the pan while still frozen, as the ice from the peas will allow them to defrost while heating up without frying. Broccoli, blanched and refreshed, can be added to the frying pan for a few minutes before serving.

- When adding peas, broccoli, or other such ingredients, you may want to use a different type of pasta. Peas, for example, will just slip through spaghetti and end up on their lonesome on the bottom of your bowl or plate, so change to penne or a similar pasta.
- You can vary the cheese: add some grated Romano cheese, or some pieces of mozzarella or ricotta.

★ Children's tip

Chopped fresh herbs can make a world of difference to a finished dish. While completely optional, they add another dimension without really needing any preparation apart from picking off the leaves and doing some chopping.

Our children have begun to love herbs such as parsley and basil on certain dishes. They add a real freshness and also, very importantly, introduce your children to these flavours at a young age. With the exception of, say, pizza, don't bother using dried herbs.

Gratin of Macaroni

I am not the greatest fan of pasta dishes containing cream. It is, however, a taste that many children adore. The one creamy pasta dish that does stand out is the Lyonnaise classic, macaroni gratin. This recipe comes from the late Alain Chapel, who was, for me, one of the greatest chefs of all and whose eponymous restaurant just north of Lyon is still one of the best in France.

One of the bonuses of this recipe is that it does not contain any flour to thicken the sauce.

You will need fresh Gruyère cheese and the best large dried macaroni that you can find; the small stuff just doesn't work the same in this dish.

Serves 4

salt and freshly ground black pepper
200g large macaroni
2 soupspoons olive oil
1 clove of garlic
200ml crème fraîche or double cream
60g fresh Gruyère cheese
10g butter

Preheat the oven to 190°C/gas mark 5.

In a large casserole, bring 2 litres of water to the boil with 20g of salt added. Add the pasta and cook for 8 minutes. Drain by lifting it out of the water and immediately coat it in the olive oil.

Meanwhile, take an ovenproof dish broad enough to fit in 2 layers of the pasta; if it is too small, the pasta will be too deep and only a small portion of it will be gratinated. Rub the inside of the dish hard with the clove of garlic, cut in half.

★ **Children's tip**

Rubbing the dish with garlic is definitely a job for the kids. They will need to be patient – when a lot of pressure is applied to the garlic it will begin to break down and cover the dish with a wonderful sweet garlic aroma. This is a classical French bourgeois technique.

In a bowl, mix the pasta with the cream and cheese. Season with salt and pepper and pour into the ovenproof dish. Dot the surface with the butter and put into the preheated oven for 10–15 minutes.

When it is done you should have a wonderful golden gratin which sure beats tinned macaroni cheese! If you want a little more colour on the top, you can pop the gratin under the grill for a minute or so.

Our son loves this!

Basic Pasta Dough

Making your own pasta is brilliant fun. Have a go.

Use a pasta machine to roll the dough. You can roll it by hand, but the results will not be as thin or even as a pasta machine gives.

The quantity of liquid used in this recipe will vary depending on the humidity and water content of the other ingredients. Use it as necessary. The level of salt is not a misprint; it will not make the pasta taste salty and will give it texture.

Put the flour and salt into a food processor and blitz for a few seconds. Add the whole eggs and yolks and blitz the mixture just until it becomes granular. Continue to blitz, starting and stopping the machine until the dough begins to come together, adding the milk as and if necessary.

Makes approximately 1kg

600g pasta flour

30g salt

3 whole eggs

10 egg yolks

a little milk (up to 100ml)

Remove the dough from the processor and, on a lightly floured work surface, knead it with your hands. You can do this by weighting down one side of the dough with the heel of one hand while stretching it away from you with the other, turning the dough as you work. Do this for 5 minutes, after which time it should feel smooth.

Wrap the dough in clingfilm and refrigerate for 2 hours. This is important, as you need to let the dough 'rest'. This allows the gluten to relax and makes the pasta less tough and easier to roll.

To roll the pasta. Working with about 150g of dough at a time, set the machine to the widest setting. Pass the dough through the machine 3 or 4 times. Now reduce the setting by one and repeat the process. Continue until you have reached the finest setting.

Rolling out the dough without using any flour makes for a lighter, less stodgy result. This method, however, is slightly trickier. As soon as you feel that the pasta is beginning to stick, you will need to hang it over the back of a chair or over a broom handle suspended between two chairs so that it dries out a bit. Take care that you do not hang it for too long or in too warm a place, or it will become too dry and will crack.

Try to get a system going where by the time that you have rolled the last ball of pasta to the first drying stage, the first ball of dough will be dry enough to continue. If you do not feel too confident about this, lightly flour the pasta when necessary. Be careful not to add too much flour, though.

When the dough is rolled to the finest setting, it will be ready to cut. Do not try to cut the pasta sheets while too moist, as they will stick to the machine; too dry and they will crack.

This pasta needs cooking for only a minute or two, no longer. If you decide to use it as lasagne sheets, make a lasagne with a pre-cooked filling that will not need too long in the oven. A delicious lasagne filling would be the oxtail leftovers (page 184), shredded up and mixed with a compote of onions (page 55).

Making your own pasta may seem like a lot of work but it really isn't. Once you've practised it a few times it will seem very easy. Let your children work at making their own pasta . . . and their own mess!

Don't forget that any extra pasta you make can be dried and used at a later date.

★ Tip

It is amazing how many people will, even when in a hurry, bring a pot of water to the boil without a lid on.

The American author Harold McGee, in his book The Curious Cook, *noted that 1 gallon of water took 23 minutes in a pan with the lid on to come to the boil from 58°F and the same amount of water took 35 minutes with the lid off. He does note, however, that the difference between a covered and an uncovered pan is only really noticeable after the water has begun to get warm and mentions that you have the time to put the water on and then go and get your lid!*

Rice

Risotto

★ **Children's tip**

One of the main ambitions of this book is to bring children into the kitchen, and one of the best ways to do this is to make cooking as approachable as possible.

So much has been written on risotto that it has earned itself a reputation as being a dish that needs a certain level of dexterity, constant attention and a wealth of experience in order to get it right. It is true that the more attention you can give to a risotto, the better the result, although it really is not difficult to make as long as you are aware of a few basic principles. With all of the ingredients to hand, your kids will be able to make a great risotto from start to finish.

As with many dishes, the best way to remove any fears about making risotto is to start with a base recipe that can then just be adapted to what you want to put in it. Most people are easily put off when, having decided that they have some of the ingredients to cook a risotto, they get a cookbook, look up a recipe and close the book again, deciding that they only have half of the ingredients after all. The point is that armed with a blueprint recipe and some basic techniques, even your children will be able to knock up a risotto after spending just a couple of minutes rummaging through the fridge and cupboards.

This approach is fundamental in giving your children greater confi-

dence in the kitchen and a real enjoyment of food and cooking. After all, none of us like doing things that we can't do very well!

One of the beauties of this dish is that, although the rice needs to be continually stirred, you can have all of your ingredients to hand and concentrate on the process of making the risotto itself.

The equipment: You will need 2 pans: a heavy-bottomed casserole in which to cook the risotto itself and a smaller one, just large enough to hold the simmering liquid. Make sure that the pan you use to cook the risotto in is not too small.

You will also need a wooden spoon, as the rice needs continual stirring. A flat-bottomed one is ideal. You can use a spatula as long as it is heat-resistant. The advantage of a flat spoon is that there is less likelihood of leaving grains of rice unmoved on the bottom and sides of the pan so that they catch.

The rice: At the Fat Duck we use a short-grain brown Italian risotto rice called superfino, although any of the risotto rice that you can buy in the supermarkets will do. These will normally be labelled 'risotto', 'Arborio', 'Carnaroli' or 'Vialone Nano'. Basically rice falls into two categories, long- and short-grain. The basic difference between the two is the quantity of something called amylopectins, the starch molecules that swell and burst during cooking, thickening the risotto. Long-grain rice has less of these and is used for pilafs, where the dish is intended to be light and fluffy. The rice used for risotto has a medium grain.

In order to maximize the breakdown of the amylopectins, small quantities of hot liquid are added to the rice while it is continually stirred.

Never wash the rice. It's an old-fashioned method that tends to remove the very thing that you need to make the dish: starch!

Always toast the rice in the pan before adding onions and garlic; it will begin to crackle and develop a delicate nutty flavour. Toasting the rice also helps to prevent the grains from sticking.

It is important to note that a risotto needs to rest for a couple of minutes before serving. You should leave it to rest when it is a little wetter than you intend serving it, as during this resting period it will soak up the excess liquid. For me, risotto should be a perfect amalgamation of rice and thickened liquid and not grains of rice in a thick liquid.

The onions and garlic: Any type of onions or shallots will be fine for risotto. They should be peeled, always making sure that the outer layers are removed, as they can be aggressive and bitter. Make sure that you chop them as finely as possible. Ideally, you want the pieces of onion to be the same size as the rice grains.

Purée the garlic with the back of a knife and a little salt as described on page 84.

The alcohol: For most risottos, a combination of white wine and Noilly Prat, or vermouth, works well. Red wine risottos are very good but are more limited in what they can go with.

The cooking liquid: Risottos are normally made using stock or, as many purists would advise, a broth in some shape or form. But do not fear: water can work quite well enough, especially for risottos using seafood such as mussels or clams, where the juices will be added towards the end. In fact, you have endless possibilities here. If you have any leftover roasting juices in the fridge, you can add them to the water if the risotto is to go with meat. You can cook the rice out in tomato juice, or add vegetables, chicken wings or herbs to the water brought to the boil and simmered. Even a tin of consommé, diluted, would be OK.

Remember that the cooking liquid should always be gently simmering when it is ladled on to the rice and that it should be added in small quantities to get the creamiest result.

The cooking oil: Butter and olive oil are normally used to fry the onions and rice, although chopped pieces of beef marrow give a wonderful richness to the dish, and, while it may sound a little strange, this is a very traditional fat to use. If all you have is cooking oil, use that along with some butter.

Finishing the risotto: Traditionally called 'mantecato', this is the point at which butter and, in the case of risotto without seafood, grated Parmesan cheese are added to the rice. This is done just before leaving the risotto to rest for a few minutes.

It is very important to beat the butter and cheese into the rice as energetically as possible. This helps to release more starch, producing a creamier finish. You can also add a little lightly whipped cream, some mascarpone or some olive oil.

★ Tip

The risotto can be made in advance and finished off at a later date. After about three-quarters of its cooking time, tip the risotto, still wet, into a fine-meshed sieve over a bowl so that you can catch the liquid. Next, pour on the remaining cold, unused liquid to prevent the rice from continuing to cook and leave until the excess liquid has dripped through the sieve. Spread the risotto out on to a tray until cold and refrigerate.

To finish the dish, put the rice back into the pan and continue to ladle on the simmering cooking liquid until the risotto is cooked.

When finished, the rice should be cooked but retaining a little resistance. Some people take the 'al dente' translation a bit literally and leave the rice grains with a chalky lump in the centre – not at all pleasant. There are many arguments about the ideal texture of the finished risotto; some areas of Italy traditionally make their risottos runnier than others. You should decide for yourselves.

Cooking times: Many recipes say that a risotto will take 18 minutes to cook. Unfortunately nothing is ever that straight-forward, and it may take longer. It will depend on many factors: for example, how long the rice has been toasted for, the type of rice itself, or slight variations in temperature. Again, with experience, you will get to know when the rice is ready, but as you will be stirring it throughout its cooking time, I suggest that you start to taste it after about 18 minutes.

The liquid itself should be boiling, but not too heavily. The secret of a good risotto is that the dish is made through a combination of the rice absorbing the liquid and the gradual breaking down or dissolving of the starchy coating on the outside of the rice itself. You do not want all of the liquid to evaporate too quickly; on the other hand, if the liquid is too cool, it will not break the starch down sufficiently.

The result will also vary somewhat, depending on what final texture you want your rice to be – it's up to you.

My Basic Risotto

This is the classic basic risotto – probably the most simple in terms of taste. It's the best one to begin with.

Serves 4

1 litre cooking liquid (water, diluted consommé, or any diluted roasting juices you may have)

75ml olive oil

400g risotto rice

2 onions, very finely chopped

1–2 cloves of garlic, crushed and puréed (see page 84)

50g unsalted butter

150ml white wine

100ml vermouth, preferably Noilly Prat

75g Parmesan cheese

1 dessertspoon lightly whipped double cream, or mascarpone

salt and freshly ground black pepper

Put the cooking liquid into a pan and bring to a very gentle simmer.

Meanwhile, heat the olive oil in a casserole until hot and add the grains of rice. Now, with your spoon or spatula, stir continuously. The rice will begin to crackle and take on a delicate nutty aroma. When this happens, add the onions, garlic and a knob of the butter. Turn the heat down to low and continue cooking for about 5 minutes. Make sure that you continue to stir so that all the grains of rice are coated in the oil.

Add the white wine and cook until it is reduced. Still stirring, add the vermouth and reduce again.

Now begin to add the hot liquid, a ladleful at a time. As soon as the liquid has all but gone, add the next ladleful, always stirring and making sure that the sides and bottom of the pan have no rice stuck to them.

After cooking for about 18 minutes, taste the rice to see if it is done. If it is not yet ready, add more liquid. If you think that you may be running out of cooking liquid, bring some more to a simmer so that you can use it as soon as you need it.

When the risotto is ready, grate the Parmesan over it and beat in the remaining butter. Finish by carefully folding in the cream, if using, and season with salt and pepper to taste. Leave the risotto to stand for a few minutes before serving.

Tomato Risotto

Follow the basic risotto recipe and, half-way through, add a couple of tablespoons of tomato fondue (see page 75). Top the finished risotto with a few confit tomatoes (see page 57) if you have any.

Pea Risotto

Make the basic risotto recipe and stir in 200g of pea purée (see page 233), 100g of frozen peas, a generous knob of unsalted butter and some grated Parmesan cheese. Add some chopped herbs (mint, parsley or tarragon) if you want and season generously. Stir this in at the last minute – too much heat will discolour the pea purée.

Olive Risotto

Make the basic risotto recipe, without the cream, and stir in some tapenade or olive purée (you can make this yourself by blanching and refreshing stoned black olives 3 times, then puréeing them). Finish with plenty of chopped basil and a little olive oil.

Mushroom Risotto

If you can get them, infuse 30g of dried cep or porcini mushrooms in your hot cooking liquid and leave to stand for half an hour before using. You will need to strain the liquid a few times before using, as these mushrooms sometimes contain quite a lot of earth and grit. Discard the mushrooms.

Finish the risotto as in the basic recipe, stirring in some mushrooms of your choice, finely chopped and sautéd in a little butter. If you want to, you can replace the vermouth with some Madeira and infuse a bunch of fresh thyme in the cooking liquid with the mushrooms.

Sprinkle on some chopped fresh parsley before serving.

Saffron Risotto

Saffron is the most expensive spice in the world. Each strand is one stigma from a crocus flower. These have to be picked by hand, and just to give you some idea of the cost of harvesting, it requires some 70,000 flowers to yield 450g of dried saffron. Saffron was harvested quite extensively in sixteenth-century England, hence the place name of Saffron Walden in Essex. The best source now, though, is Spain.

Many cheaper mass-produced products claiming to contain saffron are, in fact, given a colour boost with turmeric.

This is a classic recipe and is otherwise known as risotto milanese.

Simply dissolve two-thirds of a packet of saffron strands (do not use powdered saffron) in a tablespoon of hot water and leave to infuse for a minimum of 20 minutes. Stir this into your basic risotto just before you add the Parmesan cheese. The rice will turn a wonderful orange colour.

★ **Children's tip**
There are many recipes that require you to infuse something in a liquid. After looking into how to extract the maximum flavour from tea without the tannin, I discovered that tannin was water-soluble and not oil-soluble. Therefore by macerating tea in oil for a longer period of time, the tea flavour only was extracted.

I then learnt of an excellent way of both increasing the level of flavour extraction and also discovering which ingredients were oil- or water-soluble. This test is great to do with your children, as it gets them thinking and tasting. Simply take a sealable container and fill it with equal quantities of oil and water. Use non-flavoured, clean oil such as groundnut or grape-seed. Place in the container the flavouring of your choice: basil or saffron, for example.

Now seal the container, give it a shake, and leave it in a cool but not cold place, preferably in darkness. Every hour or so, take the container and shake it. After about a day, without shaking the container, remove the lid. You will notice that the oil and water have now separated.

Let your children taste the oil and water separately and have them consider the different flavours. Finally, shake the mixture up until the 2 liquids have blended and taste again. This will produce varying results depending on whether your flavouring ingredient is predominantly oil- or water-soluble, or, in the most interesting cases, both.

Seafood Risotto

Again, there are several variations here. You could also do a combination of all these types of seafood – mussels, clams and squid – which would be fantastic and not overly expensive.

Many traditionalists say that you must never add Parmesan cheese or cream to a seafood risotto. Why don't you and your children decide for yourselves?

Mussels: Bring some white wine to the boil with some finely chopped vegetables (onions, carrots, garlic, etc.) and add the mussels. Cook until they open, remove them, and strain and reserve the juices. Discard any that do not open.

Follow the recipe for saffron risotto, reducing the amount of saffron by half, and finish with the mussel juices.

When using mussels, remember to de-beard them first; this is just the process of pulling off the hairy stuff attached to the side of the shell.

Clams: You can do the same as above, using clams instead of mussels. Omit the saffron altogether and finish the dish with chopped fresh parsley.

There is another method for cooking clams that works brilliantly. As it does, however, involve flames, it would be best to do this yourself and let the children watch from a distance! It is based on the Spanish technique called 'a la plancha', where fish and shellfish are cooked directly on a griddle. We adapted this at the Fat Duck – we did not have a plancha griddle, so we used an iron pan.

Take a frying pan and heat some oil until smoking. Make sure that the oil is at least 1mm deep. When it is smoking, throw in the clams and shake the pan. Stand back, because when the shells begin to open, flames will flare up. Continue to shake the pan in order to keep the flames going as long as possible.

As soon as the flames have died down, pour some water into the pan and strain the juices. When you add the water, make sure that you add enough to half cover the clams, shaking the pan as the water is added. If the clams begin to spit, you can cover the pan with, for example, another upturned pan, for safety's sake.

Finish the risotto with the juices and the clams; they will have a wonderful smoky flavour.

If the pan does not ignite, it means either that your pan is not hot enough or that you need a bit more oil in the pan. Don't put too many clams in the pan at once – they will cool it down too much and prevent flaming.

★ **Children's tip**

The children will instantly find this the most enjoyable job in the kitchen! Just remember to stand well back from the flames while shaking the pan, and don't let the children get too near.

One final note on this method: if you have any fire alarms in your house, turn them off, especially if you don't want your dog to do an uncanny impersonation of Des O'Connor!

Squid Risotto

Chop up some squid and pat it dry. Heat some olive oil until smoking and fry the squid pieces for 2–3 minutes, adding some chopped chilli if you like.

Squeeze some lemon juice into the pan and mix with the basic risotto. A bunch of thyme infused in the cooking liquid would work well here.

Red Wine Risotto

Replace the vermouth with port and the white wine with 450ml of red wine, remembering the adage that if you don't want to drink it, don't cook with it!

Bring the red wine to the boil and flame it to lessen the acidity. Reduce it by half and then add it to the cooking liquid, continuing as in the basic risotto recipe.

Some sautéd smoked bacon would work well, as would flavouring the cooking water with dried mushrooms as in the mushroom risotto recipe (page 100).

Pearl Barley Risotto

★ **Children's tip**

This is an excellent way of introducing your children to a food that they might otherwise not be prepared to try.

Try using pearl barley instead of risotto rice. Just follow the basic risotto recipe (page 98) substituting pearl barley for the rice. Make the risotto up until the point where you are about to add the Parmesan cheese and the cream, if using, then take the pan off the heat and allow the risotto to cool.

To reheat, just add a little water, heat up and finish as in the basic risotto recipe.

This chapter should have given you enough ideas, but remember that as with everything, risotto-making is not written in stone. You and your children will, hopefully, develop a feel for cooking this dish and will then be able to make a risotto using whatever ingredients you have without following any specific recipe.

Couscous

Couscous is one of those ingredients that works well as a base for many different flavours and is sufficiently approachable in flavour for your children to take to it quite easily.

To make couscous, flour is sprinkled with salted water in a bowl and worked with the hands in a circular motion until it clumps into tiny little balls. These balls are then sieved to keep their size uniform and dried to form small, grain-like pieces.

Couscous played an interesting role in medieval French cuisine. In the *Vivendier*, a fifteenth-century French cookery manuscript from France, a recipe for couscous exists but is referred to as 'joke rice that is called counterfeit'.

Couscous is traditionally cooked in a couscoussier, which is essentially a form of steamer. Sometimes the stew with which it is to be served is cooked in the pan underneath the couscous. The stew can be made with chicken, lamb collar, beef shin or merguez sausage, among other things. At home you can achieve the same result by pouring boiling water over the couscous, salting it and leaving it to sit for half an hour or more, covered. It just requires fluffing up occasionally.

By toasting the couscous first, you add a wonderfully nutty flavour to it. You can then add a multitude of ingredients to create anything from a main meal to a garnish or salad. Assuming that your other ingredients are all ready, this really is fast food.

Basic Couscous Recipe

Allow 125g of couscous and 250ml of cooking liquid per person, in other words double the amount of liquid in millilitres to the amount of couscous that you will be using.

In a heavy-bottomed casserole, heat the olive oil until smoking. Add the couscous and stir continuously, ensuring that no grain remains still as it will start to catch. After about 5 minutes, the grains will take on a lovely golden-brown colour.

Serves 4

50ml olive oil

500g couscous

1 litre water

50g unsalted butter, cut into cubes

salt and freshly ground black pepper

Now is the time to add the water; but take care, as the pan will be very hot and the steam coming off the pan will be significant. As you add the liquid, stand back. After a few seconds, start stirring again. Allow the water to boil for 5 minutes or so, then remove the pan from the heat, cover and leave to stand for half an hour.

Add the butter and fluff up the couscous with a fork. Season with salt and pepper and serve. Couscous requires quite a lot of seasoning – don't be shy!

Couscous with Hazelnuts and Rosemary

Bring the water that you will be cooking the couscous in to the boil with the rosemary and simmer for 20 minutes. Leave to infuse for 10 minutes, then strain.

For every 125g of couscous:

10g hazelnuts

3 branches of fresh rosemary

If you don't have time for this, pick the leaves from the rosemary, chop them up and add them to the couscous when you add the water. (If you do this, use half the amount of rosemary.)

Preheat the oven to 200°C/gas mark 6. Coarsely chop the hazelnuts and roast them in the preheated oven for 5 minutes until they begin to brown.

Cook the couscous in the rosemary-flavoured water, adding the hazelnuts at the same time as the water.

Couscous with Ratatouille

Stir some ratatouille (see page 244) into the couscous and omit the butter.

You can also add the marinated peppers (see page 53) or the onions (see page 55) from the Snacks chapter, stir in some confit garlic purée (see page 196) or add vegetables of your choice; sautéd courgettes or aubergines would be good.

Couscous Salad

If you want to make a salad with the couscous, do not toast the grains first but pour boiling water over them and cover.

To finish the salad, mix in whatever ingredients you want, for example:

- Spring onions, diced tomatoes, diced cucumber and olives with chopped basil.
- Marinated peppers (page 53), confit tomatoes (page 57) or ratatouille (page 244).
- Chopped ginger, spring onions, soy sauce and sesame oil, perhaps with some chopped squid very briefly sautéd in hot oil.

After you have mixed in the ingredients of your choice, simply add some vinaigrette and serve.

★ **Children's tip**
As couscous is basically flour and water, you and your kids could have good fun playing around with it as a dessert: adding fresh or dried fruits, fruit purées, honey or sugar and a little cream.

Give it a go! You will be pleasantly surprised.

Soups

According to Alan Davidson in his *Oxford Companion to Food*, the word 'soup' is of German origin, coming from the word 'sup' or 'supper' and being translated in Old French to soup. Its original meaning was 'bread in liquid'. In the seventeenth century, the word 'sop' was used to describe the piece of bread that was being soaked.

Soups can be fantastic if well made. They can, however, also be pretty dreadful. One thing that you can't do is just bung everything in a pot and forget about it, as my father believes. He does not cook, in case you were wondering.

Hot soups are great comfort food for kids, whether to warm them up on a cold winter night or to soothe a poorly child. How many of us remember feeling better when given a bowl of chicken broth or tinned tomato soup?

All of these recipes, with the exception of the gazpacho and the chicken soup, are easy and relatively quick to make.

One of the important things to consider when making soup is the ingredients. Do they need to be cooked quickly in order to preserve their flavour? How thick will the soup be? What is going to thicken it? You have many ways to thicken soup: puréed vegetables or pulses, the starch from potatoes, a little cornflour or finishing with egg yolk. Any broth you may decide to make will not be thickened at all but can serve as a great medium to put other things in, such as noodles and duck, or chicken wings and vegetables.

Soups are also a great way to introduce your children to new flavours or to try to convert them to foods they might not be overly keen on.

Several of these recipes are, in effect, diluted purées of the main ingredient itself and therefore require you to buy the best quality possible. You will be amazed at the results of some of these considering their relative simplicity.

★ Tip

One very important factor in making soups, as in all savoury cooking, is seasoning. Use cayenne pepper instead of black or white, as it is more evenly distributed, being in powder form, and gives the soup a wonderful kick without making it too hot – as long as you don't add too much. Make absolutely sure that your children wash their hands after using it, even if they did use a spoon or the tip of a knife. There are parts of the body which are sensitive other than the eyes, as our son once found out!

Do not be shy with the salt. As an experiment, take some of your finished, unseasoned soup, add some salt, mix and taste again. Now keep adding more salt, a little at a time, and taste in between each addition. There will come a point where you have added too much, but unfortunately you will not know until you have done so. Remember that, as mentioned in the introduction, salt reduces the perception of bitterness. Well, this can be really beneficial when making soups. Try tasting using the squeezed nostril method (see page 20).

It is interesting to see if your children like different levels of seasoning. You will be quite surprised at the difference between salting correctly and not enough. It is probably the biggest single difference between food served at home and in a restaurant. It is also important to salt the soup while it is at the temperature at which it is intended to be served. As with sweet things, levels of seasoning change depending on temperature.

At the Fat Duck, we use tapioca in some of our soups. It is fantastic, as it adds a wonderful unctuosity to the finished soup. It works particularly well in the cream of tomato soup or the leek and potato. Tapioca is easily obtainable. Soak it for half an hour in whole milk, rinse it thoroughly, and cook it in equal quantities of milk and water until done, about half an hour or more. Just add this to your finished soup.

There are certain pieces of kitchen equipment that, although not essential, will make your life a lot easier when it comes to making soup:

A *liquidizer:* Most people these days have some form of liquidizer, even if it is only one of those small hand-held varieties, which are not overly expensive. (Do not try to liquidize anything in a food processor, you will only become frustrated!) It is important to bear in mind that although a soup will liquidize more efficiently when warm, it will not do so straight from the heat. Leave it to cool a little before blending, and make sure that the blender is left on for a decent amount of time to do its job properly.

The good old-fashioned mouli is still a good way to purée many vegetable-based soups, although unfortunately it is not as widely available as its modern-day counterparts.

A *fine-meshed sieve:* The best of these are conical in shape, with a very fine mesh. Conical sieves can generally hold more ingredients and, because they come to a point, it is easier to force your purée through. A sieve of some sort really does make a difference to the textural quality of a soup. A sturdy ladle makes pushing your liquidized ingredients through the sieve much easier and a lot quicker.

A mandolin: A mandolin is excellent for slicing vegetables very thinly for quick cooking (see page 23).

★ **Tip**

When making soups, always consider adding some lightly cooked or raw version of the same ingredient used to make the soup itself. This is a good general rule to use in cooking across the board: the butternut squash soup (page 130), for example, will be lifted immensely with the addition of very finely grated raw butternut. It creates not only a contrast in texture but a missing characteristic from the cooked butternut. Imagine generously grating butternut over a big bowl of soup at the table. It would really lift this dish!

You can do the same thing with desserts. A little raw apple grated over the tarte Tatin (page 283) will make a surprising difference.

Cream of Tomato Soup

One of the strongest childhood memories! Let your children discover the taste of a real cream of tomato soup, not the pasteurized variety sold in tins.

It is imperative that you get the best-quality, ripest tomatoes possible. As with the gazpacho recipe that follows this one, don't bother making this if all you can buy is pale, unripe, out-of-season tomatoes.

Serves 4

2kg best-quality vine tomatoes

½ onion

4 cloves of garlic

100g unsalted butter

extra virgin olive oil

I dessertspoon tomato ketchup

1 stick of celery, cut in large pieces

1 bunch of fresh thyme

500ml whole milk (this may not be necessary)

225ml double cream

salt and freshly ground black pepper

Halve the tomatoes and scoop out the seeds. Put the pulp into a sieve set over a bowl to collect the juices. Chop the flesh.

Peel and finely chop the onion and garlic. Heat half the butter and a little olive oil in a casserole and, on a medium heat, sweat the onions and garlic for 5 minutes. Add the tomatoes and their juices, ketchup, celery and thyme, bring to the boil, and simmer until reduced by two thirds.

Remove the pieces of celery and the thyme and pass the contents of the pan twice through a fine-meshed sieve, rubbing it through with the back of a tablespoon into a bowl. If you have a conical sieve, this job will be easier; force the vegetables through using a ladle. It is important that you force nearly all of the pulp through, otherwise you will lose a lot of the flavour and will be left with a bowl of insipid liquid.

Measure the liquid; you should be left with approximately 500ml. If, for some reason, you have less than this, top it up to 500ml with half water and half milk. If, on the other hand, you have more than required, return it to the casserole and reduce as necessary.

To serve the soup, simmer gently with the cream for 4–5 minutes, then, whisk in the remaining butter, and thin down with a little more milk if necessary. Season with salt and pepper.

Making Chicken in a Salt Crust with Hay – p162

Roast Wing Rib of Beef – p165

Carrots Glazed with Cumin and Orange – p214

Pea Purée – p233

Ratatouille – p244

Fish Baked in Salt – p266

Pot-roast Cod – p273

Jessica and Joy eating shellfish

Gazpacho

There are many versions of this cold soup, depending on, among other things, the region of Spain that the dish originates from and the age of the recipe. Most of us now associate this dish with tomatoes, as the main ingredient. Tomatoes, however, were not really used until more recent times; the original gazpachos were made from garlic and other vegetables such as red peppers, thickened with bread and perhaps almonds, blended with olive oil and water. These soups were, traditionally, white and not red in colour as is now the norm.

This recipe is a combination of the Andalusian version, which is tomato-based and thickened with bread, and one originating from Malaga, which is enriched with mayonnaise. It comes from a restaurant in Burgundy called La Côte Saint Jacques, which has three Michelin stars. The soup is prepared in three stages: first the vegetables are chopped up and marinated overnight in a little olive oil. The extracted juice is then poured over cubed bread, left for a few hours and strained. Finally, the soup is thickened with mayonnaise. The vinegar is very important, as the acidity brings life to the soup.

Our children absolutely love this soup – it is so refreshing. Sometimes they have bread with it, sometimes not, and they have even had it as a quick snack, drinking it out of a glass. This recipe omits the garlic, as children are not great fans of it in its raw state.

Again, as with the cream of tomato soup recipe above, the quality of the tomatoes themselves is paramount.

★ **Tip**

It is important to read the section on making mayonnaise that follows this recipe. You will wonder what all the fuss was about. Especially when your children can knock some up in a couple of minutes!

Serves 4
1 onion
2 cucumbers
4 red peppers
2.2kg best-quality ripe tomatoes
extra virgin olive oil
150g white bread
tomato ketchup
sherry vinegar
Tabasco
salt and freshly ground black pepper
For the mayonnaise
1 egg yolk
I coffeespoon French mustard
100ml mild-flavoured olive oil
100ml groundnut oil

Begin the recipe the day before you want to eat the soup.

Peel the onion, cut off the root, and chop. Peel each cucumber and cut in half along its length. Run a teaspoon along the length of the cucumber to remove the seeds, then chop the flesh.

Halve the red peppers, remove all of the seeds and pith, and chop the flesh. An easy way to do this is to slice the top and bottom off the peppers and make a vertical slit down one side. Now turn the red pepper on its side, insert the knife through the slit and run it around the inside of the pepper. This method will easily remove the pith and the seeds in one fell swoop.

Halve the tomatoes, scoop out and discard the seeds, and chop the flesh.

Put the onion, cucumbers, peppers and tomatoes into a bowl and drizzle over a little olive oil. Leave to marinate overnight.

The following day, juice the vegetables. If you do not have a juicer, put them into a food processor or liquidizer then pass them through the finest-meshed sieve available.

Break the bread up (tearing it into pieces will be fine) and add it to the vegetable juice; leave for 2 hours in the fridge to chill, then pass the liquid through a fine-meshed sieve into a bowl, making sure that you press down on the bread to remove all of its moisture. Discard the bread.

Meanwhile, make the mayonnaise. In a bowl, combine the egg yolk and mustard and whisk lightly. Gradually add the olive oil, a few drops at a time, until the mixture begins to thicken. When this happens, you can start incorporating it at a faster rate until you have used up both the olive and the groundnut oils.

When the mayonnaise is made, whisk it into the vegetable liquid. An electric hand blender is best for this job, as it will prevent tiny white specks of mayonnaise being left in the soup. Add the mayonnaise in stages, as you may well find that you only need three quarters of it. When thoroughly blended, return the soup to the fridge until cold.

This soup is best eaten at fridge temperature. If you add the finishing ingredients earlier, the acidity and sweetness will not be balanced. To finish the dish, add ketchup, sherry vinegar and Tabasco, and season with salt and pepper to taste. Do not be shy with the vinegar, just add a little at a time until you are happy with it. Let your children do this, tasting after each addition – you will be surprised how much the flavour is brought out.

★ Variation

Loads of things can be added to gazpacho to create a complete summer meal. The obvious thing would be to add chopped tomato flesh, although charred, peeled and chopped red pepper or chopped spring onions would also work well. Some fresh basil or coriander would finish the soup nicely. Crab meat, salmon (cooked or smoked), prawns or even some roasted scallops if you can get hold of them would all be good, depending on your children's tastes. We are lucky – our eldest daughter adores mussels and clams. This would also be nice with some roast chicken, which has the benefit of making the dish quite approachable for children.

Mayonnaise

Mayonnaise is one of those things that a lot of people never bother to make because they think it is too much hassle and very difficult to do – nonsense! By following a few basic principles, you and your children will be able to make it foolproof and it will take a matter of minutes.

The egg yolk plays the role of the thickening agent, as does the mustard, although to a lesser extent. It also adds flavour. Do not worry too much about how many yolks to put in; 1 egg yolk will thicken more oil than you will need. You can, if you like, replace the egg yolk with egg white. This will give a more neutral taste to the mayonnaise, which you may or may not prefer.

Salt the yolk-mustard mix, as this will thicken it in readiness for adding the oil. The mayonnaise for the gazpacho recipe uses olive oil because of the nature of the dish, but generally mayonnaise made with olive oil is too strong. Also, unrefined or extra virgin olive oils contain substances which make the emulsion of the mayonnaise less stable, subsequently reducing its shelf life. Usually the ideal oil to use for mayonnaise is groundnut, as it is unflavoured and has the benefit of remaining at the same consistency when cold.

To be on the safe side, have all the ingredients at room temperature. When making mayonnaise by hand, put a damp tea towel on the work surface and place the bowl on it; this will stabilize the bowl. Just be prepared for arguments over who is holding the bowl and who is whisking! Although it can be made in a food processor, mayonnaise really is easy to make by hand. It is also more enjoyable, and by the time you have cleaned the parts of the processor, there is very little time difference.

Choose your bowl carefully; it needs to be big enough to whisk in properly but not so big that the egg yolk simply gets lost in the bottom of it. Also, make sure that the bowl has a rounded base, otherwise some of the mixture will remain in the fold where the base meets the edge.

The whisk itself is quite important; make sure that it has enough wires on it. Some whisks have such big gaps in them that you may as well try to whisk with a fork, which will obviously not work.

Begin by adding the oil a little at a time. When it begins to thicken you can increase the amount that you add. Harold McGee, in his book *The Curious Cook*, gives a very sound piece of advice: when adding the oil, never add more than one third of the volume of the egg yolk at one time. Remember also that, to a certain extent, the mayonnaise will become thicker with the oil. Many people think that if the mix is becoming too thick, they simply have to add more oil to thin it down, finding that the opposite happens! If the mayonnaise is becoming too thick, simply add a little water. It does not need to be boiling, as some recipes advocate.

To finish the mayonnaise, add vinegar or lemon juice to taste. This is essential for two reasons; first, you need acidity to balance the richness of the oil, and second, it helps the stability of the end product. Use cayenne pepper to finish, as it gives the mayonnaise a lively character.

★ **Children's tip**

This information does away with any mystique about making mayonnaise. Your kids will be able to rustle up something infinitely superior to the bottled version in less time than it would take them to go and buy some! Just imagine: your children being able to 'knock up' some mayonnaise almost instantly because they fancy some in their sandwiches!

Leek and Potato Soup

Leeks lose their delicate flavour after only a relatively short cooking time, so this soup really does benefit from being made quickly. The ingredients need to be cut or sliced as thinly as possible; this increases the surface area of vegetable exposed to the liquid, which maximizes the flavour. A mandolin or fine slicer is ideal, if you have one. Otherwise, you have a chance to teach your children good knife technique!

The water needs to be simmering when added because otherwise it would take too long to bring it to the boil.

Cut off the green tops of the leeks, leaving the white parts. You should be left with about 750g of leek. Holding each leek flat on the chopping board, run the point of a sharp knife from about 1cm from the root end of the vegetable, all the way to the other end. Repeat this operation 3 times so that the leek is shredded at one end. Do this with all the leeks and leave them under cold running water for 5 minutes to rinse out any dirt that might be inside. Then slice them as finely as possible, making sure that all the root is discarded.

Serves 4

1kg leeks

200g onions

180g potatoes

1.7 litres water

150g unsalted butter

a bouquet garni, consisting of thyme, celery, and parsley

100ml double cream

salt and cayenne pepper

Peel the onions, cut off the roots and slice them as thinly as possible. Peel the potatoes and slice as thinly as possible, then rinse briefly under cold, running water, separating the slices.

Bring the water to a simmer. Meanwhile, in a casserole large enough to hold all the ingredients comfortably, sweat the vegetables in 120g of the butter for 5 minutes or just until the initial raw leek aroma has disappeared. Stir to make sure that all the vegetables are cooking evenly. Make sure they are not coloured at all or the flavour of the soup will be altered.

Add the bouquet garni and pour on the simmering water. Bring to the boil as quickly as possible and simmer for 10 minutes, until the potatoes are tender. They may take a little longer, especially if they were not sliced thinly enough. If they are not quite cooked, the soup will be granular. You do not, however, want the soup to cook for much longer than the 10 minutes advised, or you will lose the fresh leek flavours.

Add the cream, simmer for a few more minutes and take off the heat. Remove the bouquet garni and liquidize the soup, making sure that you leave the machine on long enough to purée the ingredients completely. Pass the liquid through your finest-meshed sieve into another bowl, or, if you are serving the soup immediately, into a saucepan. Use a ladle for this.

Season the soup with salt and cayenne pepper, whisk in the remaining cold butter, and serve.

★ Tip

A word of warning! If you are using a liquidizer, you must take a few safety precautions. As a chef, there are things in the kitchen that I tend to do without giving a thought to them. One of these is using the liquidizer to blend hot liquids. Do not pour the soup into the liquidizer, put the lid on and switch it on; you will do what my wife did and cause a leek-and-potato explosion! The hot soup went everywhere; we were eating leek-and-potato-flavoured porridge for a week afterwards!

As I mentioned earlier, you will achieve better results by letting the soup cool down a little before puréeing. The safest method is to ladle the soup into the blender, making sure that you get a good mix of solid and liquid matter and that the bowl is no more than two thirds full. Now place the lid on tightly, but – and this is a big but – leave off the smaller, inner lid so that there is a hole in the top of the blender. Gently hold a tea towel, folded over a few times (so that your hand is protected) over the opening. You can now turn the blender on.

★ **Variation**

To serve the soup cold:

   If you want to serve this cold, you will need to make the soup slightly differently, otherwise the butter will solidify and give the soup an unpleasant grainy character. Simply replace the butter with olive oil, adding a little more at the end. Remember not to season the soup until it is cold. Traditionally, this soup is sprinkled with a generous amount of chopped chives, which is not essential but is worth the effort. Cold, this becomes vichysoisse.

   To turn this soup into more of a meal, add some precooked potatoes with, perhaps, some sautéd smoked bacon and lightly sautéd leek.

Butternut Squash Soup

The ingredients for this satiny-textured soup are so few; the intrinsic sweetness of the squash itself is what makes it. It is important to use the ripest squash that you can lay your hands on and, of course, if you cannot get hold of any butternut, you can substitute one of the many other squashes or pumpkins that are now readily available.

You can finish this tasty soup with some croûtons (not cretins as my son calls them!). Some shaved Parmesan would also be delicious, so too would a few sautéd mushrooms and bacon lardons.

As with the other soup recipes, try adding some cubed butternut, sautéd so that it still retains a bite; taste the soup with and without the butternut cubes and see the difference. Some grated raw butternut would work well. This soup contains a large amount of butter, which can be reduced, especially if you are making it regularly. You should, however, try the recipe as it stands at least once.

Serves 4
1kg butternut squash
1 large onion
200g unsalted butter
1 litre water
700ml whole milk
salt and cayenne pepper

If you want to add an extra dimension, prepare half of the butternut as directed in the recipe and roast the other half, brushed with olive oil, until lightly browned and soft. Both butternuts can then be combined just before blending.

Peel the butternut squash using a peeler, cut it in half lengthways and scoop out the seeds, then slice the flesh as thinly as possible, using a mandolin if you have one.

Halve the onion and cut off the root. Then peel the onion and slice it as thinly as possible.

Take a casserole large enough to hold all the ingredients and melt 150g of the butter. Add the onion and butternut and sweat over a low to medium heat for 10 minutes, then turn the heat up, add the water, bring to the boil and simmer for 30 minutes or until the vegetables are completely soft.

Remove from the heat, liquidize the soup in a blender, then pass it through a fine-meshed sieve. You now need to thin this liquid with the milk, adding enough to obtain the correct consistency and checking that you are not diluting the flavour too much.

To finish, reheat the soup gently in the casserole, whisk in the remaining butter, check the seasoning and serve.

Lentil Soup

If possible, make this soup with the slate-green coloured Puy lentils, which have the best flavour. They are more expensive than ordinary lentils, but in terms of this recipe the extra cost is not much compared to the increase in quality.

The vegetables have been kept in bigger pieces so that they can be easily removed before the lentils are puréed. Leaving them in would remove much of the taste and textural character of the lentils themselves.

The vinegar is optional but does balance the soup wonderfully.

Peel and crush the garlic. Halve and peel the onion; leave the root on and stud with the cloves.

Top and tail the carrots; peel them and cut each one into quarters, lengthways. Cut off the green part of the leeks, trim off their roots and cut across in half so that they will remain intact during cooking. Cut the root off the fennel to separate the layers.

If using one piece of bacon, cut it into 3 or 4 pieces. If using rashers, leave them as they are.

Put the lentils into a large casserole, cover with cold water, bring to the boil, drain, and refresh under cold running water. Put them back into the casserole and add all the vegeta-

Serves 4

2 cloves of garlic

1 onion

3 cloves

2 carrots

2 leeks

1/2 a small head of fennel

75g smoked bacon, in one piece or in rashers but not cut into lardons

250g Puy lentils

a bouquet garni consisting of rosemary, thyme, bay leaf and celery leaf

1 litre water

salt, freshly ground black pepper, and cayenne pepper

whole milk to taste

150ml double cream

50g butter

a few drops of sherry vinegar or balsamic vinegar (optional)

bles and the bouquet garni. Cover with the water, bring to the boil and simmer for 40 minutes or until the lentils and vegetables are soft. Salt the lentils 5 minutes from the end of their cooking time. Be careful not to over-salt, as some of the cooking liquid will be used to make the soup.

Strain the lentils, reserving some of the cooking water, and discard all the vegetables and the herbs. Liquidize, adding some of the reserved cooking water if necessary. Pass through a fine-meshed sieve into another pan.

Heat gently, gradually whisking in the milk until you have the desired consistency. Whisk in the cream and finally the butter. Finish with the vinegar, if using, and salt, pepper and cayenne to taste.

The bacon which was cooked with the lentils can be diced and sautéd and added to the finished soup. If you like, you can remove a handful of the whole cooked lentils before you purée them and add them to the soup at the end.

The addition of lightly cooked, finely diced vegetables (the same kind used in making the soup itself) will give it an extra dimension.

★ Children's tip

My children love this soup, so I thought it would be a good way to introduce them to chicken livers. I thinned the soup less than in the recipe, so that it had more of a sauce consistency, then sautéd some fresh chicken livers that had been soaked in milk for half an hour. I gave the kids sautéd chicken livers with fried bacon and onions and a lentil sauce, and they really enjoyed it.

It is still the only way that we can get them to eat chicken livers!

Chicken Soup

An essential addition to any Jewish household.

This recipe calls for chicken wings, as they are inexpensive and easily obtainable, but you can use carcasses or a whole chicken. The amount of vegetables is important to give a rounded flavour. Celery gives a nice fragrance to the soup, but its inclusion will tend to lessen the time that the soup will keep in the fridge.

This recipe yields a clear soup with a lot of flavour. The vegetables are chopped finely and are added to the soup in such an order as to preserve their flavour without giving a stewed note to the end result.

There is also a supplementary recipe, using this base to cook more vegetables and chicken that will be retained in the final soup.

Put the chicken wings into a casserole, pour over cold water just to cover and bring to the boil on a high heat. As soon as the water boils, skim off any impurities that may have risen to the surface, lift out the wings and cool them under running water; pat dry.

Peel and finely chop the onions, garlic, carrots and celeriac. Finely slice the mushrooms.

On a medium heat, melt the butter, add the chicken wings, onion, garlic, carrot, celeriac and mushrooms, and cook for 15 minutes.

Makes 1 litre
1kg chicken wings
2 large onions
2 cloves of garlic
3 large carrots
1 small head of celeriac
250g button mushrooms
100g unsalted butter
3 sticks of celery
3 leeks
a small piece of fresh ginger, peeled
200ml dry white wine
a bouquet garni consisting of thyme, bay leaf and celery leaves
4 whole star anise
salt and freshly ground black pepper
1 large bunch of fresh parsley

While the wings are cooking, prepare the other vegetables: finely slice the celery, and remove the green of the leek, finely slice it, and add to the celery along with the peeled ginger. Set aside.

Turn the heat up, pour in the wine, bring to the boil and reduce by half. Pour over cold water to cover by 5cm, bring to the boil, skim off any impurities that may have risen to the surface, add the bouquet garni and star anise, and simmer for 45 minutes. It is important that the liquid stays at a very gentle simmer and does not boil at all, otherwise any impurities that may rise to the surface will be driven back into the soup, making it cloudy and bitter. Do not worry about skimming off any fat that rises, as it will automatically rise to the surface when the finished soup is left to cool and you can then easily remove it by placing a sheet of kitchen paper on top and lifting it off; the paper will take most of the fat with it.

After 30 minutes, add the leek/celery/ginger mix. After 45 minutes, turn off the heat; season if necessary, add the parsley and leave to stand for 20 minutes.

Strain the soup through a fine-meshed sieve and then, if you have some, muslin.

★ Tip
Muslin is very good for fine straining. You need to make sure that the cloth is rinsed under the cold tap and wrung out just before you use it. It will help trap any fine impurities.

This soup can be eaten straight away, or left to cool and kept in an airtight container in the fridge.

To finish this soup off, after the 45-minute simmering, you can add basically whatever you want to, bearing in mind that some vegetables take longer to cook than others. For example, potatoes should go in shortly before carrots, and vegetables like green beans, leeks and lettuce should be put in much nearer the end.

You can also add pasta or noodles and pulses such as haricot beans or lentils.

Other flavourings such as lemongrass would work well; as would some onion compote (see page 55) which can be used to finish the dish.

Finally, don't forget herbs, as they can really transform even the most unexciting soups. Basil, for example, puréed or in the form of pesto, makes a great addition to the above recipe – stir it in at the end.

You obviously do not have to follow this recipe by the book – it can be adapted according to your taste and the amount of time that you and your family have available. Try to remember the following points:

- If you want maximum flavour from your soup while preserving the individual characteristics of each of the ingredients, cut the vegetables as small as possible to maximize their surface area.

- If you are planning on eating the vegetables separately that have been cooked in the soup, cut them into slightly larger pieces.
- Try to keep the soup as seasonal as possible: use root vegetables in the winter and vegetables such as peas and broad beans in spring.

Sunday Lunch

Although I work Sunday lunches at the Fat Duck, the restaurant is closed in the evening. It is the one time each week that we, as a family, can guarantee to spend together around the table without having to rush off somewhere. My most eagerly anticipated moment of the week is arriving home from work late in the afternoon on Sunday to a frenetic and excited welcome (and that is just from my wife!).

Generally, Sunday lunch tends to be the meal that the whole family can prepare together and where the children can learn the pleasures of cooking and the table. It is so important to move away from the image of the family sitting around the dinner table in silence, gazing vacantly at a television screen. Sharing a meal round the table together has to be one of life's greatest pleasures, and children are only going to appreciate this if they are treated as adults and involved as opposed to the 'seen and not heard' attitude commonplace in the past. Children who are made to feel part of the lunch or dinner table and do not dread these mealtimes will grow up to enjoy not only the food but, equally important, the social gathering, whether friends or just family.

The purpose of sitting around the table is primarily to eat the food, but it is this that creates the platform for younger people to begin to develop their self-confidence, be it talking about their own interests or listening to other people's. It is during these meals and the preparation of them that you, as a parent, can help to widen your child's understanding of food.

★ Children's tip

Now here is a subject which might be contentious, and perhaps a little delicate: children and vegetarianism.

It is important that children make their own decisions about what they will and won't eat, whether this is on moral or taste grounds. It should be our responsibility, as parents, to make sure they have all the information they need to be able to make this decision. We must not pass any of our own eating hang-ups on to them. I have always made our children aware that, for example, when they are eating beef, they are actually eating cow. There is nothing wrong with this as long as the animal has led a good, healthy life and has been killed humanely. The quality of the end product is directly influenced by the quality of life of the animal itself. After all, evolution has designed us to be carnivorous both in the way that we eat and the way that we process our food.

Unfortunately, supermarket price wars have resulted in all food prices, including that of livestock, coming down over the last couple of years. If we would only stop to think: how is this possible? Land and property values and wages are increasing. Inflation still exists. How then can meat and poultry prices fall? On the face of it, the answer is through more efficient farming. That is a constructive use of the word – 'efficient' should be replaced with 'intensive'. In many cases, farmers have little choice if they are to compete in the market of livestock trading. Animals are being packed together, fed on a diet of low-cost feed, hormones and antibiotics. What life are these animals leading? Their own immune systems are so low that they are unable to properly fight disease themselves, and the conditions that they exist in are a breeding ground for all sorts of bacteria. The recent epidemic of foot and mouth disease might not have been so widespread if the animals had had full use of their own self-defence mechanisms.

Because of the reduction in the number of slaughterhouses in this country (there are currently fewer than 350 compared to 1,500 a year or so ago), the animals must now travel further in cramped lorries to be killed. This will have also contributed to the spread of the foot and mouth virus, as well as creating unnecessary stress to the animals themselves.

If one good thing can result from the epidemic, let us hope that kinder farming practices will evolve and that the farmers themselves will be able to survive financially in following them.

In this chapter I have included dishes that are both delicious to eat and ideal for this time of the week, as everyone can get involved in a relaxed atmosphere. There is nothing like the aroma of Sunday roast filling the house. Although this may sound like rather a sweeping statement, for me Sunday lunch will always consist of the main attraction: a fantastic joint of free-range meat, or a wonderful bird, which will yield precious juices for the gravy, plus the essential roast potatoes and at least two other vegetables, all put on the table so that everyone can help themselves.

It is mainly for this reason that there are no fish dishes in this Sunday lunch chapter. To a large extent it's a personal thing, but I feel that it's easier to introduce your child to eating fish gradually with snacks or evening meals than at what may be the biggest meal of the week. You can always serve something fish-based as a starter or snack beforehand so that the children are not put under any pressure; if they do not want it, no problem.

All the recipes in this chapter are for the main dish. The recipes for the garnishes are in the vegetable chapter (see page

191), so that you can decide for yourself which ones to serve, if any.

Over the last couple of years, I have done a lot of work on low-temperature cooking and in particular, the important temperature thresholds in meat cookery. Lean pieces of meat are traditionally subjected to very high temperatures for relatively short periods of time in order to achieve a far lower core temperature in the meat itself, but why not cook the meat at a temperature far closer to its final desired core?

The important stages in the cooking process of meat are as follows:

- From 40°C, meat proteins begin to contract until, by the time they have reached 60°C, they begin to force moisture out and by the time they reach 70°C most of the precious, moist juices have gone, leaving a grey, dry piece of meat.
- From 55°C, collagen, the stuff contained in meat, bones and muscle, begins to break down. Prolonged exposure to this temperature will render this gelatinous and give the meat tenderness without making it dry. Up to a certain point, the longer the exposure, the more collagen will be broken down. The age of the animal will also have an effect; the younger the animal, the lower the temperature at which the collagen will gelatinize. This means that the meat will take longer to cook but the end result is fantastic.
- At 100°C, the water contained in meat (up to 75 per cent) evaporates. This must be avoided, as the meat will become totally inedible.

The only downside to cooking at these lower temperatures is that the desirable browning flavours on the outside of the meat are not obtained. This can be overcome by giving the meat a blast in a hot pan before or after cooking.

As a rough guideline to the extra cooking time required with this technique, it will take, for example, some 3 hours to cook an 8cm thick piece of lamb or beef to the rare stage at an oven temperature of 75°C.

After you have got the hang of these recipes and the basic principles involved, try experimenting by reducing cooking temperatures. The results of cooking meat at lower temperatures for a longer period of time are incredible, and noticeably superior to cooking at higher temperatures for a shorter period.

This method does, however, have its drawbacks: it takes a long time, needs an accurate probe (see page 26) and not everyone has a double oven. The double oven allows, for example, the roast potatoes to be cooked at their required temperature while the meat is gently cooking in the other oven at a much lower temperature.

The importance of both an oven thermometer and a digital probe cannot be stressed enough. These 2 pieces of equipment are not at all expensive (see page 339 for where to buy them).

Cooking meat this way means that the method of allowing a certain number of minutes per pound is not necessary. As mentioned earlier, it is also nonsense, as a piece of meat twice the thickness of another will, in fact take four times as long to cook. Also, two ribs of beef may both have the same thickness. One rib may, however, be twice the height of another and hence twice the weight. If the thickness is the same, both ribs will cook in the same length of time.

It may not be feasible to cook your meat at low temperature, so I will give alternative methods where appropriate. It would be interesting to try them both anyway. The children can get involved in checking temperatures, keeping an eye on the meat and getting to know what they should be looking for: for example, if you are trying to cook a piece of meat at a low temperature and you can see juices in the pan that were not there when the meat went in, the temperature has got too high, squeezing precious juices out of the meat itself.

In summary, here are the main pros and cons of low-temperature cooking:

Pros:
- This method produces the most wonderfully tender and succulent meat; you will be amazed!
- Using lower temperatures, a digital probe and an oven thermometer, you will obtain almost foolproof and consistent results.
- As no residual heat has been built up you are effectively cooking the meat at its ideal serving temperature.

Cons:
- Because most of the juices are still in the meat, there is little in the pan with which to make a sauce. This means that, if you want some gravy, you will have to make it separately. You can still use whatever is in the roasting tray, of course, but it will have to be supplemented by an additional sauce. I have given a relatively simple method for great gravy and one that can be used as a blueprint for meat sauces.
- The meat is not being cooked at temperatures high enough

to develop those wonderful browning flavours caused by a complex chemical process called the Maillard reaction. You can combat this to some extent by subjecting the meat to a very high temperature (the maximum that your oven will reach) for the shortest possible time until some browning has taken place.

• This method does require time and patience, but as long as you have the right equipment, it really is just waiting time as opposed to preparation time.

★ **Tip**

The way that we carve meat can play a vital role in how we perceive its tenderness. As mentioned in the roast leg of lamb recipe, the meat should be carved across the grain. This means that when you are eating the meat, your teeth bite down on the fibres, easily separating them and giving the perception of tenderness to the meat. If the meat is cut along instead of through the fibres, your teeth will have to bite across them. This will make the meat appear to be less tender, causing you to chew more. This in turn will cause a dryness in the mouth that will make the meat less juicy than biting down on the fibres. Cut the same piece of meat in the two different ways and make the test with your children to see what they think.

It is very important always to consider food hygiene, particularly in the handling of meat. Although many people think food poisoning results from bacteria in the food itself, in many cases it is a result of bad hygiene in the handling process and cross-contamination: for example, touching meat or placing, say, a vegetable that may be intended to be eaten raw on a surface that has just had some raw chicken placed on it. Fastidious care and attention must always be taken when handling food. This discipline also gives your children vital awareness and teaches them to work in an orderly manner. For example, always try to perform one stage of a job to the finish before starting the next stage. So, if you are peeling and slicing carrots, finish peeling them all and discard the peelings, cleaning the surface before you start slicing them. Not only does this help to eliminate cross-contamination, but it also creates an orderly working environment where you and your children can work without ending up in complete chaos!

It seems really obvious, but one of the most common sources of infection comes from not washing hands between jobs – a particular example would be first cutting up chicken then preparing fruit or vegetables.

There is a contact address on page 339 for further information on this subject.

The importance of teaching your children to buy the best quality meat available, from retailers who really do care about where their meat comes from and how it has been butchered and handled, cannot be emphasized enough.

I believe that we should not have to be told to overcook our meat and poultry and hard-boil our eggs. There is a risk element to many things that we do in life and, as consumers, we have the freedom to make our own choices, not only in how we cook our food, but also in how we choose and handle it.

What would life be if we were banned from making mayonnaise with wonderfully fresh free-range eggs, or prevented from feeding a child on wedges of hot buttered toast dipped into fabulous creamy free-range egg yolks? What about something as simple as a chocolate mousse made with yolks and whites? If we were denied the right of choice, all of the world's greatest cheeses would be banned for containing unpasteurized milk. Even being offered the choice of how we want our steak or lamb cooked would disappear, as it would all have to be very well done.

We live in a society where we are able to choose what we feed on. Arming ourselves with the best information about the origins of our food, both in quality and morality, then reinforcing this with secure and fastidious handling, will provide us with some of the most delicious ingredients that we can eat. Remember that not only is it difficult to cook first-rate food using second-rate ingredients but it is also possible to turn a free-range animal into bad meat by careless handling.

We, as parents, have to make our own decisions about what we and our children eat, in the knowledge that, albeit very small, certain risks are involved. Many of us do not have the money to live off fillet steak and lobster and why should we want to anyway? A shoulder of lamb or a shin of beef from a healthy free-range animal is far cheaper, and gives us a fantastic opportunity to learn to cook with our children, invariably producing tastier, more satisfying results.

The importance of resting meat

A good friend of mine looked at me in complete bewilderment when I told her that the meat was resting, and said, 'Poor thing, are you going to make it a cup of tea as well?' But leaving meat to rest for a certain period of time after cooking is as important as the cooking itself.

Briefly, what happens when meat is cooked is as follows: the heat penetrates the meat from the outside in (except, of course, in the case of a microwave). At higher temperatures, the juices near the outside of the meat are forced out. Resting meat allows it to cool down, and to continue to cook at the same time with the heat that has built up in the meat tissue itself. The contracted fibres will gradually 'relax' and allow the juices to spread out evenly through the meat, resulting in a more tender texture with better taste.

An unrested piece of meat will have a brown-grey band around the outside and a definite line of colour change on the inside. A piece of meat that has been rested, however, will be an even colour right the way through. Even when cooking meat at low temperature a good resting period will ensure that your meat is more juicy.

Many people who like their meat well done just don't want to see blood, which is quite understandable. In fact, it is not actually blood: this is removed at slaughter. It is juices held in the meat that contain substances that exist in blood, giving it its red colour when heated.

As a rule, a 2.5–3kg joint of beef cooked at a conventional temperature will require a minimum of 1 hour of resting, preferably longer; even at lower temperature allow 30 minutes. If the meat after resting is a little too cold, just give it a quick blast in the oven or under the grill; it will only take a couple of minutes.

Tenderness and flavour

The relationship between tenderness and flavour in meat and poultry is very important. The tenderest cuts of meat are not always the most flavoursome. Likewise, completely free-range meat will, in general, be slightly less tender than its mass-produced counterpart, as the free-range animal will be fitter and more muscular.

What is guaranteed, however, is that the healthier, fitter animal will taste far better. The same can be said for different cuts of meat from the one animal, depending on how lean it is. A fillet of beef, for example, will be tenderer than, say, the sirloin but will actually have a less pronounced flavour.

At the restaurant, we use a breed of chicken from the Bresse region of France, which is a pure breed, living on a diet of milk, maize and worms in a completely free-range environment. It is the king of all chickens, and so it should be at the price! What is quite striking is its appearance: it has very elongated breasts that are thinner than our supermarket chickens and the meat itself is tougher to eat. The most shocking moment, however, comes when you taste it. It is then that the difference between pure, organic, artisan farming methods and the ones that produce what we as consumers are fed nowadays becomes apparent.

Unfortunately all of this comes at a cost, and most of us cannot afford such luxuries. Everyone should try, within his or her price bracket, to obtain the best ingredients that they can afford. We owe it to our children.

Pot-roast Pork

This method of cooking, generally known as 'en cocotte' in French cuisine, can be adapted to many different meats: chicken and other poultry, duck, lamb, etc. It incorporates browning, roasting and braising and generally favours the larger cuts of meat: racks, leg joints and whole birds. Pot-roasting requires the meat to be almost baked in a sealed container along with a small amount of liquid, creating a wonderful sauce which is, in essence, the juices of the meat – pure and not masked by any stock. The meat can be cooked with a whole range of aromatics: vegetables, herbs and spices, even a little fruit or other cuts of meat, raw or cured, and the technique also works very well with fish.

Too often people are put off by the thought of having to make a stock before they even begin to think about the recipe itself. Here the domestic cook has an advantage over most restaurants, in that some of the best sauces are made from the browned pan juices – one chicken will, for example, give enough juices for 4 portions of sauce. At the Fat Duck we roast whole birds and joints of meat just to yield small quantities of pure and concentrated meat juices. This method is too costly for many restaurants, but is actually cheaper to do at home as the sauce is merely a by-product of the meal itself.

This brings me on to one of my pet hates. If you have ever eaten in a restaurant with any form of gastronomical intention, you may have noticed the word 'jus' on the menu. This word is normally prefixed with words such as 'Madeira', 'thyme', or even in some completely ludicrous cases 'raspberry' or 'port wine' (instead of 'port'). These sauces are nearly always made from reducing veal stock with other aromatics and finishing with the relevant flavourings. One problem with this type of sauce-making is that even if well made, the veal stock tends to make most of these sauces taste the same and a little gelatinous. The other problem is that they are not jus. A jus is the deglazed juices from a piece or pieces of meat and not the reduction of a stock. As mentioned before, this is where the home cook is lucky, for the juices rendered from a joint of meat cooked conventionally, and not at low temperature, are sufficient to produce enough sauce for that joint and far better than the more time-consuming method of making a stock and then drastically reducing it.

This dish does need to be started 2–3 days in advance, but you will be amazed at the results. You will never have tasted pork quite like this before!

★ Variation

Salting the pork is not essential, but it really does heighten the flavour. If you are short of time or inclination, simply omit the whole process of salting and studding the meat. You could then add a couple of sage leaves to the pan just before putting it in the oven.

This recipe allows you to put the skin taken off the pork back into the oven at an increased heat to crisp into golden crackling. There is, however, a fantastically simple way to make crackling. Just take some raw skin, put it on a plate and stick it in the microwave on full power! Within minutes, you will have crisp and light crackling. If it is not crisp enough, just give it a little more time.

Serves 4

1 × 4-rib rack of pork, free-range if possible, taken 2 ribs back from the best end (just ask your butcher, he will understand, honestly!) – the reason for this is that the first couple of ribs-worth of meat are too lean

a little salt and freshly ground black pepper

For the cure

1 large bunch of fresh thyme, leaves picked

200g salt

1 clove of garlic

salt and freshly ground black pepper

1 bunch of fresh sage, leaves picked

For the glaze

3 egg yolks

2 tablespoons honey

2 tablespoons Indonesian soy sauce

For the cooking process

1 large onion

2 medium/large carrots

1 leek

3 cloves of garlic

150g unsalted butter

50ml groundnut oil

1 bunch of fresh thyme

1 bunch of fresh marjoram (optional)

2–3 days in advance. First make the cure. Chop the thyme leaves, mix them with the salt and reserve.

Peel the cloves of garlic and cut into matchstick-thick batons, making sure that you have at least 18 of them. Blanch them in water for 1 minute, then drain and refresh. Repeat this process twice and pat dry.

Put some salt and freshly ground pepper in a small ramekin, using approximately 1 teaspoon of salt to $\frac{1}{4}$ teaspoon of pepper, and add the garlic batons. Mix well, then wrap each baton in a small sage leaf. Reserve.

Now take the piece of pork and turn it upside down so that you are looking at the flat, bony side. With a small pointed knife, make 2 parallel rows of incisions, about 1.5cm deep, and insert a sage-wrapped garlic baton into each one. Still working on the same side, make 3 similar incisions in the fat that connects the skin to the meat, inserting the garlic as before.

Turn the rack so that you are looking down on the ribs and again make 2 rows of holes, in between each rib. Stuff these with garlic batons as before. Finally, turn the rack so that it is sitting on its flat side and you are now looking down on to the top of the bones. Make the last 3 incisions into the fat that runs alongside the skin, and stuff with garlic batons.

This process is far easier than it sounds; the important thing here is to get 18 sage-wrapped batons into the meat evenly, sticking them not deep into the meat but into the fat or against the bone.

Once you have done this for the first time, you will not do it again . . . only joking! It will seem so simple the next time.

Now, on the work surface, lay out some clingfilm, large enough to wrap around the pork twice. Cover an area about the same size as the meat with about half of the herbed salt and place the pork, skin side down, on it. Cover all of the sides except for the exposed meat ends with the rest of the salt and carefully wrap the joint twice in the clingfilm. Make sure that the salt stays in position. Put the joint into the fridge.

After 2 days, thoroughly wash off the salt and pat the meat dry.

On the day of cooking. Preheat the oven to 160°C/gas mark 2.

Peel and quarter the onion and carrots. Cut the root and green off the leek, cut into 4 lengths and wash. Chop the garlic.

In a lidded casserole big enough to fit the joint, melt 100g of the butter with the groundnut oil over a moderate heat. When beginning to colour, add the pork and lightly brown on all sides. This browning process is important, as it will give a stronger, richer flavour to the sauce. Remove the pork and, if necessary, replace the butter if too brown.

Now lightly colour the vegetables and garlic and place the pork on top, skin side down. Add the herbs. Put the lid on the casserole and place in the oven.

To make the glaze, whisk all the ingredients together and set aside.

After the pork has been cooking for about 25 minutes,

remove the casserole from the oven and turn the pork over. Return it to the oven for another 25 minutes, then remove the casserole from the oven again, take out the pork, and put it on a board. Turn the oven up to 220°C/gas mark 7.

With a sharp knife, carefully remove the skin from the pork, taking care to leave as much fat on the meat as possible. Score this fat by running a knife through it in a criss-cross pattern, ensuring that you do not go into the meat itself, and allow the meat to rest until you have made the sauce.

To make the sauce, place the casserole on a moderate heat and allow the vegetables to cook to a lovely golden brown. Pour off the excess fat. Add about 300ml of cold water, bring to the boil, and simmer for 20 minutes. Strain into a smaller pan and, if necessary, reduce a little to reach the desired consistency. Set aside. Discard the browned vegetables.

To finish the dish, generously brush the fat with the glaze and return to the hot oven until nicely caramelized. This should take approximately 10 minutes. You can, if you wish, put the skin in the oven for crackling. When the pork is ready, remove it from the oven and put it on a board. With a long, sharp knife, cut down and across against the contour of the bone to leave just the piece of meat.

Collect any juices that may have come out of the meat and add to the sauce. Finish the sauce with a knob of butter, gently whisking it in.

At the table, cut the pork into thick slices and serve – fantastic.

Roast Chicken

Rather than a specific recipe for roast chicken, here are some points which will give the best results.

The benefit of an oven thermometer cannot be emphasized enough. You may be surprised at just how inaccurate your oven is! For details of where to buy one, see page 339.

1. Choose the best chicken that your budget will allow. Always remember that it is the quality of your ingredients that will play the biggest part in determining the end result.

2. Season the bird generously inside and out with salt and freshly ground black pepper.

3. Cut off any extremities such as wing tips, feet and neck; roughly chop them and add to the roasting tray. This will form the base for your sauce. If you can, remove the wishbone by lifting up the flap of skin covering the neck cavity. Using a small, sharp knife, run the blade along the wishbone on each side of the V-shaped cavity. You should be able to ease this away from the breastbone and carefully pull it off the chicken. When you have done this once, it will be easy.

Removing the wishbone makes the chicken far easier to carve and minimizes the amount of meat left on the carcass.

4. You can, if you wish, stuff the cavity of the chicken with a lemon (pierced with a fork and rolled with some pressure on the work surface), a clove of garlic, or herbs such as thyme, rosemary and tarragon. This is a good exercise for the kids, as it will enable them to see later if they can taste any of the ingredients stuffed into the cavity prior to cooking. They will also have more experience through touching and smelling and will be able to learn some valuable food hygiene regarding the handling of raw chicken.

It is quite surprising how many people, quite rightly, are fastidious over hygiene concerning the handling of raw chicken but will never think about washing hands after handling fresh eggs (still in the shell). The outside of the eggshell can have as much bacteria as the raw chicken itself, for obvious reasons.

5. Tie or truss the chicken. This is important, as it keeps the bird in a compact shape and helps maintain an even cooking.

6. Any aromatics added to the pan will greatly enhance the quality of your sauce, the most important being onion, garlic and herbs.

7. Do not cook the chicken on too high a heat. You have a couple of choices here. Armed with a probe or accurate thermometer (see page 26), cook the chicken at 75°C until the internal temperature has reached 65°C. Then remove the chicken, turn the oven to the highest heat, and give the bird a blast, just until the skin is browned. However, although this will give you fantastic results, the chicken will retain all of its moisture, and the problem with this is that as all of those precious juices are inside the bird, there are none in the pan from which to make the sauce.

At the restaurant, we would make a separate sauce or roasting juice to accompany the chicken. The chances are that you won't want to be bothered with that. So, a happy medium needs to be found.

Cook the chicken at 140°C/gas mark 1 until done. Basically, you have many options and variations of cooking times and temperatures, and although it may seem like a bit of a minefield to many of you, but just remember that you will be looking for an internal temperature of 60–65°C, and that the higher the temperature that you cook the chicken, the more residual heat will be produced. This means that when your chicken has reached the desired temperature, this residual heat will continue cooking the bird, even out of the oven!

Also, if you are cooking the bird at a higher temperature, the breasts will cook at a different rate to the legs. To overcome this, cook the chicken for a third of the time on one leg, a third of the time on the other and the final third of the time resting on its back (so that the breasts are facing up).

As a rough guide, at 140°C a 1.5kg chicken will take approximately 1 hour to cook: 20 minutes on each leg and 20 on its back.

It is important to note that some older ovens may be hotter at the back than the front. In this case, make sure that the chicken is placed in the oven with the thicker end of the breast towards the back. While on the subject of ovens, as they become older and more used, a carbon-type build-up can form on the walls. Although the oven may well be regularly cleaned, there could be some less shiny spots. This matt surface will absorb heat instead of reflecting it, meaning that the oven will not have an even, consistent temperature. You can combat this by using a clay dish with a tall fitting cover. This is then preheated and put inside the oven, creating, as it were, an inner oven that will have a uniform temperature in which to cook the chicken.

9. When the chicken is cooked it will need to rest. Place an upturned small bowl on a bigger plate and rest the chicken against it so that the thinner part of the breast is pointing up. This way, the juices will flow back to the thicker part of the breast and any juices will be kept. Cover with tin foil and leave to rest for at least 30 minutes.

10. As with the pork recipe (page 153), you just have to brown any pan juices, bones and aromatics, add water, approximately 300ml for a chicken, simmer for about 30 minutes and strain, reducing if necessary. Finish by whisking in a knob of cold butter.

This process of adding liquid to a roasting pan is called deglazing and is where a flat-bottomed wooden spoon would come in handy for scraping up those precious juices squeezed out from the meat when cooked at higher temperatures.

So, that's it! Oh, one very important point, don't forget to have a tussle over the best part of the chicken: the oysters. These are the little nuggets of super-rich dark meat attached to the backbone of the chicken. In France they are called 'sot l'y laisse'. This means 'Only fools leave them'.

And by the way, if you have not yet read the introduction, there are a couple of medieval recipes on page 32 that should help show you what not to do; although the kids might find them interesting!

Chicken in a Salt Crust with Hay

Traditionally, in parts of Burgundy and around Lyon in France, whole legs of ham used to be cooked in hay. It gives the meat a wonderful farmyard flavour. At the Fat Duck we cook sweetbreads in hay, wrapped in a salt crust pastry, which, in effect, causes the meat to steam inside as the hard crust forms.

You can buy a bag of hay from any pet shop; it is very inexpensive. Make sure that you buy hay and not straw; it is sometimes sold as meadowsweet hay. A probe (see page 26) will remove any uncertainty about whether or not this chicken is cooked inside its golden crust.

First make the pastry. Finely chop the herbs and, with the exception of the water, mix all the ingredients together. Add enough water at the end to bring the dough together. You do not want this to be too wet, or, on the other hand, too dry, or it will be too crumbly and will fall apart.

Now, on to kneading. You can use a mixer with a dough hook, or, alternatively, do this by hand. This is a very dense dough which will require kneading for at least 10 minutes – which is why you might want to use a machine. Wrap it tightly in clingfilm and leave to rest in the fridge for at least 2 hours. It is

Serves 4

hay, about a carrier-bag full (it is probably easier to describe the quantity this way than for you to have your whole kitchen covered in hay trying to weigh it; believe me, it gets everywhere!)

1 lemon

1 bunch of fresh thyme

1 chicken, weighing about 1.5kg

For the salt crust pastry

50g fresh thyme

50g fresh rosemary

1.6kg strong plain flour

700g salt

480g egg white (about 15 egg whites)

370g water

always important to rest dough otherwise it will shrink and toughen during cooking.

★ **Children's tip**

Kneading is a great exercise for children as they can, with experience, learn about textures of dough and begin to understand the difference between those for breads, biscuits and pastries. It is also very relaxing, if you can get your child to do it for long enough. Unfortunately, some children have a very short attention span!

Soak the hay for at least a couple of hours in cold water, preferably overnight, and squeeze dry. This accentuates the hay flavour and the slight moisture will aid the steaming process. It will also, believe it or not, make it easier and less messy to wrap up the chicken.

On a floured work surface, roll out the dough to a thickness of about 0.5cm and place a mound of damp hay in the middle. The pastry should be 20–25cm bigger all round than the chicken and hay inside.

Roll the lemon back and forth on the work surface with the palm of your hand and pierce it several times with a fork. Season the chicken inside and out with pepper (no salt, as the bird will take on some salt from the pastry during cooking) and stuff the lemon and the thyme into the cavity. Place it upside down on the hay. Cover it with more hay and wrap the dough around the bird so that it comes together and completely seals it in. It is very important that there are no holes in the pastry, as the crust will act as a steamer and you do not want to let any of the steam out.

Cook the chicken in the oven at 220°C/gas mark 7 for about

40 minutes. By this time, the pastry should have become hard and lightly brown.

Remove from the oven and leave untouched for 35 minutes. Now take the chicken to the table and open the parcel, but take care, as the interior may still contain a little steam!

Carve the chicken. If the legs are still a little undercooked, finish them off under the grill or return them to the oven, skin side down, for a few minutes. Rub the pieces with butter and serve.

This dish is cooked at a high temperature, as the pastry needs to form a crust so that although the chicken is being roasted, it is actually steaming inside the crust. The wonderfully delicate flavour of the chicken almost plays second fiddle to the fragrant aromas escaping when the crust is broken.

When the salt crust is opened at the table, everyone gets the initial impact of the parcel, followed by the incredible aroma along with the fantastic sight of the chicken nestling in its bed of hay. What a wonderful feast!

★ Variation
You can, if you want, put fresh rosemary, bay or thyme in with the hay. If you are going to do this, make sure you use a lot of it.

★ Children's tip
The children will love this – it's like an episode of 'In the Kitchen with Blue Peter' and 'Down on the Farm' all rolled into one!

Roast Wing Rib of Beef

I absolutely love roast beef. It is, in many ways, the quintessence of an English Sunday. It conjures up a morning of reading the newspapers after a nice walk with the dog, and then off to the pub to see your drinking mates while the dinner is cooking. Arriving home to the wonderful aromas and a major ear-bending!

As with any ingredient, the most important concern here is the quality of the beef. The meat should be deep red and marbled with flecks of slightly yellow fat. Even with the farcical beef on the bone ban, we chefs could buy and cook beef on the bone as long as it was served off the bone! This made absolutely no sense whatsoever. It was as much a politically fuelled panic reaction as anything else.

At last this fiasco is over and we can now buy our ribs, bones and all. The bad news is that many supermarkets still insist on selling boneless ribs. This is ridiculous! The bone acts as both a conductor and a protector. And it makes a great addition to your meltingly tender roast if you put the bone with the little bits of meat still attached to it back under the grill until brown and crisp – the mixture of crisp brown with the more pink tender pieces is fantastic.

★ Tip

A word of warning: if your rib is boneless, scrunch up some tin foil and use it as a pillow on which to rest the meat on in the roasting tray while it is cooking. If the joint has no bone to protect it against the direct heat of the roasting tray, even at lower temperatures it will dry out and cook unevenly.

Meat and fish always taste much better cooked on the bone. But many supermarkets now sell as beef on the bone a piece of meat with a 10cm rib bone loosely attached to it which serves little purpose whatsoever. If you can buy the meat from your butcher, ask for wing rib, on the bone with the chine still attached. This is the bone that the roast will sit on while cooking.

You should always try to get completely free-range meat. There are many butchers that specialize in this, giving you and your children the knowledge and comfort that the animal has led a healthy life, been humanely treated, and that the quality of the meat will be assured.

This recipe has given two versions, conventional and low-temperature. Why not try them both and see what you think?

Many books advise cooking your meat by weight. This theory would not be foolproof even if the increased weight of a joint of meat was in proportion to its increased size. A piece of meat twice the thickness of another will take four times as long to cook.

The other problem is that although the joint of meat could be twice the weight of the one you last cooked, it may well be taller and not much thicker (most of its extra weight coming from its height). Obviously the same calculation would not then work, as the time taken for the heat to penetrate to the centre would be shorter.

Although it is important to bear in mind cooking times, do not treat them as foolproof.

It is important not to become too obsessed about exact quantities. There can be significant differences in size of ribs, particularly when buying from the butcher. It is really important that you and your children develop the confidence to buy and cook using the senses. Choose a piece of meat with good fat marbling and a deep red colour, preferably a slightly dryer look to the flesh and the fat on the outside slightly crumbly. Choose the size by sight, for if you approach ingredients this way with your children, you will not become a slave to recipes but will instead be cooking from the heart.

Remove the meat from the fridge a couple of hours before roasting, as this will enable it to cook more evenly.

Preheat the oven to 160°C/gas mark 2.

Heat the butter in a casserole on a medium to high heat, and when it begins to turn brown, add the meat, unseasoned. If possible avoid using a non-stick pan, as you actually want all the precious browned juices and proteins to stick to the bottom, creating your sauce. While the meat is browning, baste it by pouring the foaming butter over the beef. This helps to brown the other side quicker and also delays the point at which the butter will get too hot and burn. Both sides of the meat should be browned as quickly as possible so that the aggressive heat of the pan does not penetrate the meat too much.

When both sides are nicely browned, turn the meat upright so that it is sitting on the flat chine bone and let this colour.

Serves 4

1 × **2-bone wing rib of beef, from the sirloin (ask your butcher for any off-cuts that he might have – these can go in the pan to add to the flavour of the sauce. If you are buying your meat from the supermarket, the piece should be 7.5–10cm thick)**

150g unsalted butter

1 carrot, chopped

1 onion, chopped

1 clove of garlic, chopped

any spare beef or veal rib or chine bones that you can get hold of

350ml beef juice from the following recipe (this is obviously optional. If you have neither the time nor the inclination to make this, replace with water)

salt and freshly ground black pepper

Once this has been done, pour off the butter if burnt and add a little fresh butter, making sure that you do not lose any precious juices.

Add the chopped vegetables. If you have any bones or off-cuts, put them into the pan now for a few minutes before the meat goes into the oven. Tip out the excess butter and generously season the meat. Put the beef in the oven, still upright, and cook for 21 minutes per kilo (remember, this is just a very rough guide). A probe (see page 26) will make life a lot easier.

★ Tip

The only reason for browning meat is the flavour that the browning process gives to both the meat and the resulting sauce, or gravy. It does not, as some people believe, seal in all the juices. If browning was necessary to do this, then poached beef or chicken would be really dry instead of wonderfully tender.

Also, when meat is browned, we are left with bits in the pan that we use to make the sauce; these juices have come from the inside of the meat. Basically, if we heat meat tissue up enough, the fibres will contract and with the increasing temperature will force more juices out of the meat.

If you take 2 pieces of steak, exactly the same size and cut of meat, and cook one to the rare stage and the other so that it is very well done, making sure that both of these steaks have been browned, the very well-done piece will be noticeably smaller than the rare one. This is because precious juices have been forced out, leaving the meat more dry and shrunken.

When the meat is done, remove it from the oven, season it again, and allow it to rest for 10–15 minutes on a rack over another pan or bowl so that you can catch all the juices. While the meat is resting, pour off the excess fat from the roasting pan, taking care to keep any precious juices, and return the pan to the top of the stove to brown the vegetables and meat trimmings. When the bottom of the pan has become deep brown (take care not to let it burn!), deglaze it by pouring in some water and scraping up all the juices with a wooden spoon.

You can add some chopped onion or shallots to the pan just after the meat has been removed and colour these along with the pan-juices and other vegetables.

Beef juice (300ml, from the recipe on page 172) could be added, or chicken soup if you have some. Alternatively, just add water and gently reduce this to a sauce consistency. Another option is to deglaze the pan with 10ml of port and 250ml of red wine. If doing this, ignite the alcohol with a match as soon as it boils; first do this to the port, reducing it by half before adding the red wine and repeating the process. Then add 300ml of water and reduce to taste.

★ **Tip**
Flaming does not necessarily alter the actual acidity but it does alter the perceived acidity. For example, vinegar mixed with honey will be as acidic as vinegar on its own but it will seem less so.

When you are ready to eat, return the meat to the oven for a few minutes, no longer, just to reheat it.

To serve, keep the meat upright (in the same position as it was cooked) and, with a sharp knife, take the meat off the bone. Stand the piece of meat upright so that the cylindrical 'eye' of the meat is running parallel to the front edge of your work surface and slice across the grain. This will ensure that the meat will feel at its most tender in the mouth.

Finally, pour over the slices any of the juices which have come from the resting and carving of the meat, then season again and serve. Pouring these juices over the meat accentuates the tenderness and is preferable to pouring them into the pan, as the juices coagulate and do not really add much to the sauce itself.

Roast Wing Rib of Beef, Low-temperature Version

1 × 2-bone wing rib of beef
groundnut oil
100g unsalted butter
salt and freshly ground black pepper

Preheat the oven to 75°C/gas mark ⅛.

Generously season the beef and wipe with the oil. Place in the roasting tray as in the previous recipe, and cook until the internal temperature reaches 52°C. Please be patient, this will take at least 2 hours! Don't succumb to the temptation to turn the oven up.

When the meat is ready, heat the butter in a frying pan on the stove until it starts to turn brown and is still foaming. Remove the beef from the oven and place in the pan. Cook for a few minutes, basting continually. When one side has browned, turn the meat over and do the same on the other side.

Carve as in the previous recipe.

If you have the inclination, pour out the butter and add 300–400ml of the following beef juice recipe.

It really is not that much bother and is well worth the effort.

Beef Juice

Place the chicken wings in a casserole, cover with cold water and bring to the boil. Reduce the heat and simmer for 5 minutes.

Tip the contents of the casserole into a colander over a sink. Discard the water and generously rinse the wings under the cold tap. Put back in the rinsed-out casserole and add fresh cold water to cover.

Put the casserole on the heat, bring to the boil, then turn the heat down to a simmer. Add the rest of the ingredients and cook at a very gentle simmer (the odd bubble rising to the surface) for 1½ hours, then strain through a fine sieve or damp muslin if you have some and set aside.

For the chicken broth
750g chicken wing tips, chopped
1 onion, peeled and quartered
1 carrot, peeled and cut into eighths
1 stick of celery, trimmed and cut into quarters
1 white of leek, cut across into quarters
3 cloves of garlic, bashed
1 bunch of fresh thyme
½ fresh bay leaf (optional)

In a casserole, heat half the butter and a dessertspoon of the oil. When hot, add the meat and cook, stirring regularly, until lightly browned.

Tip the contents of the pan through a colander and put the remaining butter with more oil back into the pan. Add the onion and anise and cook until the onion begins to soften. Add the rest of the vegetables and cook until lightly browned. Put in the meat and cook for 5 minutes more.

Now add a ladleful of the chicken broth and stir with a wooden spoon, scraping up all the brown bits. When the liquid has completely reduced, repeat the process. Continue doing this 3 or 4 more times until the meat is covered in a syrupy coating. Add the rest of the broth and the herbs, if using, and cook on a gentle simmer for an hour or so.

Strain the liquid into a smaller casserole and if necessary reduce to the desired consistency. A little cold butter can be whisked in at the end.

For the beef juice

50g unsalted butter

groundnut oil

750g shin of beef

1 onion, peeled and thinly sliced

1 star anise

1 carrot peeled and thinly sliced

2 cloves of garlic, bashed

chicken broth (see above)

fresh herbs (thyme, rosemary, etc . . . optional)

Roast Leg of Lamb

We can now buy fantastic quality lamb from all over the UK. At certain times of the year, for example, lamb from the Outer Hebrides is available. This animal has fed on heather and gorse in the sea air. It is a gastronome's treat!

Personally, I am not a big fanatic of milk-fed lamb. Although very tender, its pale flesh yields almost too mild a taste. It is from about 4 months old that the taste begins to develop.

Some recipes advise studding the meat with garlic or other things such as rosemary and anchovies. The problem with this is that first it detracts too much from the delicate flavour of the lamb and second, by doing this, the meat is pierced, allowing precious juices to escape. If you really want to insert garlic into the lamb, you can stuff it between the meat and the bone without penetrating the flesh at all.

This recipe subjects the meat to a more conventional temperature but if the time and equipment are available, cook the lamb at the lower temperature of 70°C until the internal temperature reaches 55°C. This will take about 2^1/$_2$ hours.

If the lamb is going to be cooked at the lower temperature, the garlic will not be cooked sufficiently, so it can be left out. There will also be almost no juice in the pan with which to make a sauce. You can make a separate sauce or, if you don't have the inclination to do this, adjust the garnishes accordingly. For example, ratatouille with lamb is so fantastic that it does not need a sauce to go with it.

One thing is for sure, however. Cooked at the lower temperature the meat will be unbelievably tender and juicy.

Serves 6

1 × 2–2.5kg leg of lamb
salt and freshly ground black pepper
olive or groundnut oil
a small bunch of fresh rosemary and
a small bunch of fresh thyme
1 bulb of garlic

Preheat the oven to 170°C/gas mark 3.

Season the lamb with salt and pepper, rub with the oil, and place in a roasting tray on top of the rosemary and thyme.

Slice the top off the bulb of garlic to expose all of the cloves and place it face up in the roasting tray. Splash a couple of tablespoons of water over the meat and garlic.

Place in the preheated oven and cook for approximately 40 minutes per kg; please remember that this really is only a guideline in the absence of a probe.

While the lamb is cooking turn it in its juices every 15 minutes. This serves two purposes: it means that the meat is cooking evenly, as the heat from the pan will be more direct than the heat from the oven, and that the juices will be richer, producing fuller-tasting gravy. From time to time, sprinkle a little water over the garlic to stop it from roasting too much and becoming bitter.

Remove the meat from the oven, season again, and leave it to rest in a warm place following the same method (page 169) as for the beef, catching any juices that may have escaped, for at least 1 hour. While the meat is resting, add about 150ml of water to the roasting tray, making sure that the garlic gets a sprinkling of water.

Return the tray to the oven for 20 minutes, then remove from the oven. Take the garlic out of the pan and break off 4 of the cloves. Remove the skins from them and return these to the roasting tray. Put the rest of the garlic to one side ready to make the garnish.

Place the tray on a medium heat, allowing the juices to brown lightly. Pour in 400ml of cold water and, using a flat-bottomed wooden spoon, scrape the bottom of the pan and gently crush the garlic cloves in the roasting tray. This will give a wonderfully sweet garlic aroma to the sauce.

Return the meat to the oven if necessary for 10 minutes to reheat before serving. When carving, always carve across the grain and not along it, as the meat will be more tender and juicy and there will be less wastage (see page 147). This means that the meat should be carved by cutting down to the bone as opposed to along it. This should, in general, apply to most meats.

Pour over the slices any juices that have come out of the meat while resting, and garnish with the rest of the garlic cloves. These are delicious, pushed out of their skins and spread on the meat or a piece of bread.

Seven-hour Leg of Lamb

This is an adaptation of a famous French bourgeois dish called 'Gigot de sept heures' – ideal for people who cannot bear to eat meat with any trace of blood-like juices in it.

The star anise in this dish works as a flavour enhancer rather than a spice flavouring. In combination with onion it will enhance the taste of the lamb itself. This technique works with any meat dish, although it is important to note that the star anise needs to be sweated with the onion otherwise instead of the anise and onion in combination creating a meaty character, the flavour of the anise itself will dominate. Try it with the following recipe, or the oxtail recipe on page 184. This technique is not exactly new; the Chinese have been using it for several hundred years!

Although it is called seven-hour leg of lamb, this really is the shortest time that you should cook it for. Ten to twelve hours would be great! This slow-cooked leg is also delicious cold, in sandwiches or as a salad with some olives, goat's cheese and a little vinaigrette.

★ **Variation**

A fantastic addition to the lamb, if you have the energy, is first to gently cook 2 very finely sliced onions in 75g of butter for half an hour and set aside. Next, peel and very finely slice 3 potatoes and rinse the slices in water.

About 2 hours before the lamb is ready, carefully remove it from the pan and tip the contents into a fine mesh sieve set over a bowl. With the back of a spoon, gently press on the vegetables to extract all the juices. Spread the onions on the bottom of the roasting tray and cover with the sliced potatoes, overlapping them evenly. At this time you will probably need to add 150ml of water. Make sure that the liquid is poured over the potatoes, although they do not have to be covered in water as they will cook through the hot, moist vapour in the pan.

Place the meat back on top of the potatoes and continue with the recipe. If you are adding this garnish, turn the oven up to 80°C/gas mark a little above 1/8 otherwise the potatoes will not cook.

For this recipe, you will need an oven tray big enough to hold the lamb and the vegetables. Although the dish should have a lid, tin foil will work quite effectively. If you do use tin foil, make sure that as little vapour as possible can escape during cooking.

Two days before cooking, rub the meat with half of the Maldon salt and half the thyme.

On the day of cooking, wipe any excess salt off and brown the leg in olive oil in a casserole with a tight-fitting lid. Pepper the meat and set aside, leaving the oil in the casserole.

Preheat the oven to 70°C/gas mark 1/8.

Peel and roughly chop the carrots and onions. Pour out excess fat from the casserole, add the vegetables and star anise, and cook until lightly brown, adding a little fresh olive oil if necessary.

Spread the vegetables in the roasting tray and put the meat

Serves 6–7

1 × 3kg leg of lamb

30g Maldon sea salt

10g fresh thyme

olive oil

salt and freshly ground black pepper

2 carrots

2 onions

1½ star anise

1 bulb of garlic

a bouquet garni consisting of a bay leaf and generous amounts of fresh thyme and rosemary

300ml white wine

100g unsalted butter

2 tablespoons chopped fresh parsley (optional, but really does make a difference)

on top. Cut the bulb of garlic in half horizontally, and place half each side of the meat. Add the bouquet garni and 300ml of water to the pan and put the lid on.

Place the pan in the preheated oven and cook for at least 7 hours. Every half an hour or so, remove the tray from the oven and baste the meat with the juices in the pan, adding more water when necessary. It is important to maintain the level of the water during the full cooking time. Half an hour before the meat is ready, add the rest of the thyme.

While the lamb is cooking, put the white wine in a saucepan over a medium heat. As soon as it comes to the boil, flame by holding a naked flame to the liquid; just watch your fingers! Reduce the wine until thick and syrupy, to about 50ml.

Carefully remove the leg of lamb from the roasting tray and set aside. Put a fine-meshed sieve over the saucepan containing the reduced wine and tip the contents of the roasting tray into the sieve. Press on the vegetables with the back of a spoon to extract all of the juices, and discard the contents of the sieve. Bring the sieved mixture to the boil and reduce if necessary, skimming off any impurities that come to the surface. When the liquid has reduced to a sauce consistency, whisk in the cold butter. If you have added the potato garnish (see page 178), you will have already discarded the vegetables and will simply need to lift the potatoes out together with the onions, using a slotted spoon, and tip the juices in the roasting tray through the sieve on to the reduced wine.

Put the lamb on top of the potatoes, if using, sprinkle with the parsley, if using, and serve with the sauce on the side.

There is an expression in France that describes meat as tender as this. It is 'à la cuillère' or 'with a spoon'. One word of warning, however. If, as an English person, your French is not the greatest, take care: 'à la couelle' refers to a male animal's privates!

★ **Children's tip**

Our children adore this dish. It has the added benefit of filling the house with wonderful aromas for hours before lunch. The kids love to baste the meat themselves as it means that they can tear off and eat morsels of meat as they do so.

Braised Shoulder of Lamb

Not too dissimilar from the previous recipe, this is a rustic dish that is, again, very simple to do.

★ Tip

When cooking meat, it is important to understand what part of the animal a particular cut has come from. Is it a part that has had to do a lot of work? Or one that has remained pretty idle? The amount of connective tissue or collagen that exists in a particular piece of meat will determine the way that it should be cooked. As I have mentioned, muscle proteins begin to denature when the temperature passes 40°C. As the temperature passes 50°C and nears 60°C, these proteins coagulate and, in effect, become tough. Therefore lean cuts of meat such as fillet should be cooked to 55°C (60°C would be the absolute maximum). When cuts have more connective tissue, such as shin, oxtail and shoulder for example, a different approach needs to be taken. The tough, hard connective tissue needs to gelatinize so that it provides a melting richness to the meat. This, however, does not start to happen until the temperature is above 55–60°C and the meat needs to be subjected to the necessary temperature range for some time (several hours).

With cuts of meat containing more connective tissue, a balance needs to be drawn between cooking the meat at a temperature that will convert the gristly connective tissue into unctuous juicy pieces of meat and one that will also not overly toughen the muscle proteins. I feel that the range of 60–70°C is about as good a balance as possible, remembering that the nearer it is to 60°C, the longer the time the meat needs to be cooked. It's useful for children to understand the basis of this theory and to be able to relate cuts of meat to different cooking processes, to think about why this is so and which part of the animal these cuts come from.

Serves 6

salt and freshly ground black pepper

1 × 1.5–2kg shoulder of lamb

extra virgin olive oil

2 medium onions, peeled, halved and roughly chopped

1 bulb of garlic, cut in half crosswise

fresh rosemary and thyme

350ml white wine

Preheat the oven to 70°C/gas mark ⅛.

Season the meat and liberally cover in olive oil. Place in the roasting pan with the chopped onions and add the garlic and herbs. Put the roasting pan over the heat and brown the meat and vegetables lightly. You may want to add a little extra olive oil.

Remove the meat and vegetables from the roasting pan while you deglaze it by adding the white wine and scraping the pan with a wooden spoon. Bring to the boil, then put back the meat and vegetables, cover the roasting pan with tin foil and place in the preheated oven.

After about 45 minutes, remove the tin foil and if necessary add more water, so that you have about 1cm of liquid in the bottom of the pan. Continue cooking for another 5 hours, again adding a little liquid if necessary and basting the meat occasionally. After this time, you will have the tenderest piece of meat imaginable. Remove the meat from the pan so that you can finish the sauce.

All you need to do now is to add 300ml of water to the roasting pan and gently reduce to a sauce consistency. You do have some options here. You can, for example, add some chopped black olives, no more than 2 salted anchovies, washed, and some fresh herbs such as basil at the end. You can even stir in a little grain mustard; it is up to you. When your sauce is just beginning to thicken, strain it through a fine mesh sieve into a small saucepan and reduce until you have the desired consistency.

Carefully carve the meat into 2cm thick slices and serve. This is another dish that can be eaten with a spoon. Maybe I am longing to return to my childhood!

Braised Oxtail

This recipe is by no means quick – you will need to start 2 days before you want to eat it! It's a long recipe, but most of the time involved is waiting time. It does have the advantage, though, that it can be prepared in advance and finished off very easily. As with the lamb shoulder in the previous recipe, oxtail contains a lot of connective tissue and needs to be cooked for a long time to gelatinize the collagen.

The amount of red wine may seem large, but it is necessary for the richness of the dish. Remember, if the wine is not good enough to drink, do not cook with it. You can also try this recipe without the 24-hour marinade. Simply follow the recipe without leaving the meat to marinate. It will be interesting to see whether or not you think that the difference is worth it!

It is important to use a casserole large enough to hold all the pieces comfortably, otherwise it will be difficult to lift the delicate pieces of oxtail out of the cooking liquid when finishing the dish.

2 days in advance. Two days before you want to eat this, prepare the marinade. Place the spices, orange zest and black pepper in muslin and tie into a bag (not essential, but it just means that your children will not be chewing on peppercorns!).

Peel the carrots, top and tail them, and cut them into quarters (in half lengthways and widthways). Peel and quarter the onions. (Keeping the vegetables in larger pieces will make it easier to remove them later.)

Take a large casserole and put it on a medium heat. Sauté the carrots in 50g of the butter with about the same amount of oil. When they begin to brown, after approximately 30 minutes, add the onions and continue cooking until they too have become golden brown.

In the meantime, chop the leek and celery and add to the casserole with the carrots, onions and the bulb of garlic, sliced in half crossways. Cook gently for another 10 minutes, then stir in the tomato purée and cook for 5–10 minutes on a high heat, stirring regularly, until the tinned tomato purée aroma disappears and is replaced by one of a nutty richness. Remove from the heat and set aside.

Finely slice the mushrooms and sauté them in 75g of the butter until they have released all of their liquid and become nicely brown. Drain off the excess fat and add the mushrooms to the carrot and onion mix.

Take a casserole large enough to hold all the tomatoes in one layer, pour a film of oil over the bottom and place the tomatoes cut side down over the base of it. Place the casserole on a medium heat and leave the tomatoes to brown. You will not need to move them at all and will be able to see dark brown edges forming on the outside of the tomatoes. At this point pour in the sherry vinegar

Serves 6

2 star anise

5 cloves

10 allspice berries

zest of 1 orange

1 teaspoon cracked black pepper

6 carrots

6 medium onions

175g unsalted butter

groundnut oil

4 large leeks

1 head of celery

1 bulb of garlic

100g tomato purée

350g white button mushrooms

6–8 ripe tomatoes, halved

100ml sherry vinegar

200ml white wine

2.5kg oxtail, jointed (ensure you are not given lots of small, tail-end pieces)

2 tablespoons plain flour

salt and freshly ground black pepper

200ml port

1.5 litres red wine

a bouquet garni consisting of a bunch of fresh thyme, 12 fresh bay leaves and 5 sprigs of fresh rosemary, tied together

15g sugar (unrefined if possible)

150ml red wine vinegar

and stand back; otherwise you will feel as if someone has just sprayed horseradish up your nose! When all the vinegar has boiled off and reduced, pour in the white wine, bring to the boil, and with your trusty flat-bottomed wooden spoon scrape the bottom of the casserole. When the wine has reduced and you are left with a syrupy mush at the bottom, scrape it on to the other vegetables.

Now take the oxtail pieces and toss them in the flour, making sure that you shake off all of the excess. Season the oxtail pieces. Heat about 2mm of groundnut oil in a casserole, add the oxtail pieces, and brown them over a high heat. Ideally, you will want to do this in 2 or 3 batches so that each piece will be touching the bottom of the casserole, allowing you to get a nice even browning. If necessary, change the oil in the casserole so you are not trying to brown the meat in burnt oil. Once you have browned all the meat, remove it from the casserole and add to the vegetables. Leaving the casserole on the heat, pour in the port, bring to the boil, and as soon as the liquid boils, flame it. Reduce by half, add the red wine and repeat the process, once again reducing by half. (Please note that the alcohol will be difficult to ignite unless it is boiling.) Make sure that you scrape the bottom of the casserole with your flat-bottomed spoon to loosen any bits stuck to the bottom.

Add the spice bag and the bouquet garni, boil the liquid for 5 minutes, then set aside to cool. When it has cooled to room temperature, pour it over the meat and vegetables. The pieces of meat will need to be covered by about 1cm. If there is not enough liquid for this, add some cold water.

Leave to marinate for 24 hours in a cool place.

On the day of cooking. On the day you want to cook it, pre-heat the oven to 75°C/gas mark 1/8. Transfer everything to a casserole and set it on a high heat. Bring the liquid to the boil, making sure that the bottom of the casserole is scraped to prevent anything from sticking. As soon as it boils, skim off any impurities that rise to the surface. Remove from the heat, place a cartouche (see page 50) on the surface of the liquid and put the casserole in the oven. Cook for a minimum of 7 hours, checking occasionally and topping up with water if the level of liquid has dropped too much.

After about 3–4 hours, you need to remove the vegetables from the casserole – at this stage the oxtail will be less tender and will not fall apart in the process. First carefully lift out the pieces of oxtail and place them on a tray (with sides to catch any juices that may run out). Now pour the liquid through a fine-meshed sieve into a bowl. Press down on the contents of the sieve to extract the juices. Discard the contents of the sieve. Keep the bouquet garni and spice bag and return them to the pan.

If you have some muslin, moisten it with cold water and pass the liquid through a double layer of this. If not, pass it once more through the fine-meshed sieve. Put the oxtail pieces back in the casserole and cover with the liquid; top up with water if necessary and continue cooking in the oven for the remainder of the 7-hour period.

Many books will tell you, when simmering like this or making stocks, to skim the fat from the surface regularly. This is unnecessary. Fat holds flavour and will add to the flavour of the stew. It is better to remove the fat towards the end of the cooking time – and if the casserole is put in the fridge the fat will rise to the surface and can easily be skimmed off anyway.

After 7 hours the oxtail will be wonderfully tender. Remove the casserole from the oven and set aside. It is better to leave the meat to cool down in the liquid before removing the pieces of oxtail – if you remove them too soon, they will tend to dry out as they cool. Make sure, however, that the stew is not too cold or the pieces of oxtail will stick together.

Reserve about 150ml of the liquid and reduce the rest on a medium to high heat until you are left with about 400ml (if, for some reason, you do not have enough for this, top up with cold water).

Meanwhile, cook the sugar in a small saucepan on a high heat until it begins to brown (be careful not to let it burn). Now pour in the red wine vinegar but stand back, as it will create a lot of steam. Reduce this liquid down to a syrup and immediately add the reduced cooking liquid, again pouring it through a fine-meshed sieve. Bring back to the boil, skim again, and reduce until you have your desired sauce consistency. To reheat the oxtail, place the meat on an oven tray and pour over the reserved cooking liquid. Bring to a simmer on the stove and then place in the oven at about 70°C/gas mark 1/8 for about 40 minutes, basting with the liquid to keep the meat moist.

★ Tip

When reheating braised dishes, some care does need to be taken. All the loving care and attention that has gone into the preparation of the dish can be ruined by reheating it in a hotter environment than it was cooked in originally. On the other hand, fastidious care must be taken to reheat the dish sufficiently to prevent spoilage by bacteria.

If there is not enough liquid to baste the dish, add a little water.

Transfer the meat to a serving dish and pour the cooking liquid through the sieve again on to the sauce. Reduce to the desired consistency and whisk in a couple of knobs of cold butter. Pour this over the oxtail and serve.

Phew!

This may seem a very lengthy recipe but it is not as complicated as it looks, believe me. The extra steps will show in the end result. Too often a recipe for a stew ends up with tough, dry meat in a watery tasteless sauce. This is not the case here.

★ Variation

You can prepare this even more in advance if you like! Once the meat is cooked, removed and the sauce strained, you can pour it over the meat and reserve in the fridge. Once cool, you will easily be able to scrape off any fat from the surface. To finish, reheat the stew gently, removing the meat when warm, and follow the recipe to its conclusion.

If, after all of this, you still have the energy, some cooked carrots would make a nice accompaniment, as, of course, would mashed potato.

Vegetables

Although most of us will have fond memories of crunching on raw carrot or a stick of celery, this may be one area where your children will begin to turn up their noses. Finding one or more vegetables that all your children can eat may sometimes feel like having to rewrite *War and Peace* in Greek!

From personal experience, letting your children get involved in preparing the vegetables goes a long way to solving this problem. Even if they are not over-fond of the end result, there will be more likelihood of persuading them at least to taste them.

Vegetables present many jobs for children: from peeling to chopping, picking to washing, seeding to soaking and puréeing to cooking. It is important, though, to begin at the beginning and involve them first in choosing the raw ingredients. Take your children around a supermarket, greengrocer, farmers' market or farm shop and show them the different varieties of vegetables and herbs that are now available. Help them to understand the difference between organically grown produce and genetically engineered or irradiated vegetables that may look great but have absolutely no flavour whatsoever. Show them the difference between a genuine organic ingredient and an intensively grown one – for example, between a red pepper that is twisted and slightly brown and one that is almost symmetrical and perfectly red.

Over recent years, supermarkets have increased tremendously

the variety of ingredients available to the consumer. They have, however, become too powerful, in some respects almost brainwashing us into believing that the less blemished and the more perfectly shaped a fruit or vegetable, the better it is. Not 'the better its flavour will be', as this element of marketing seems almost to have taken a back seat. Sales of organic vegetables are increasing rapidly and the supermarkets are capitalizing on this. There are also many farms now that operate an organic vegetable service, where the customer can have a regular supply of organic produce delivered to his or her door.

Another aspect of fruit and vegetables is what is in or out of season. Thanks to the combination of airfreight and modern farming methods, we can now eat strawberries at Christmas, tomatoes all year round, and many other cultivated foods at just about any time of year that we want to. When our parents were young, the seasons had far more effect on what could be found in the shops than they do today. We cannot let our children grow up with the only barometer of seasons being the weather. After all, even those of us who lived in a built-up area of London can still remember going for a walk with our parents and picking blackberries for a blackberry and apple pie. These tastes conjure up memories far greater than the taste itself, a lasting memory of my childhood that I would never want to be without.

In the early days of the Fat Duck, some customers asked why there were no separate vegetables with their dishes. I tried to explain to them that we probably spend more time preparing vegetables than anything else.

The French, Spanish and Italians give more respect to vegetables than we in this country do. They use them more constructively, turning them into dishes in their own right rather than producing a plate of mixed, steamed or boiled vegetables with a knob of butter on top as we do. In fact, our reputation this side of the Atlantic when it comes to vegetables is such that the French have a terminology in cooking called *à l'anglaise*. When vegetables are cooked in this manner they are boiled! Of course, if you have the chance to eat the best, freshest asparagus in season or tomatoes straight off the vine you will need to do very little to them in order to experience something wonderful.

This chapter provides many recipes that the children can be involved in. This will hopefully get them to eat more vegetables and discover the immense versatility that they offer without having to re-create something that you as a parent might have been served up at school!

Confit Garlic

This is a great base preparation that can be made in fairly large quantities and kept in the fridge, covered, for several weeks. It is very useful to have on hand to add to many dishes. It can be mashed or blended to a sweet garlic purée that can be spread on toast or mixed with, for example, tuna in a salad Niçoise; you can finish sauces with it, stir it into mashed potato, or use it to make gratin dauphinoise.

Place some peeled garlic cloves in a pan and cover with whole milk. Bring to the boil, and as soon as the milk has boiled, drain the garlic and cool down under the cold tap. Repeat the process 4 times, using fresh milk each time.

★ **Children's tip**
It may seem a little ridiculous, but this process gets rid of the aggressive aromas. If it really is too much hassle for you – and let's face it, anything that will test the patience of an adult will certainly do the same for the younger members of the family – leave it out. The difference will be that the unblanched garlic will be harsher. Why not try each method and see if the difference is worth it? Get your kids to take part in the experiment.

Wash the garlic cloves and dry them thoroughly. Put them into a pan and cover them with olive oil. If you like, you can add fresh herbs such as rosemary, thyme or bay leaf.

Now either put the pan on a low heat, or cover it and place it in the oven for a couple of hours. It is important that the temperature of the oil does not exceed 70°C, otherwise there is a risk that the garlic cloves will begin to fry and become bitter.

When done, the garlic cloves should have retained some of their whiteness. They will be really soft and have a wonderfully sweet taste. To store them, keep the whole cloves in the oil, in the fridge; just take them out as and when they are needed.

Cooking Green Vegetables

This method can be applied to all green vegetables – the only variation is the cooking time. However, this recipe relates to green beans, as they are one of those vegetables that is either very overcooked, turning a lovely muddy brown colour and tasting as though they have come from a tin, or completely undercooked, looking vibrant green and tasting, well . . . of nothing much at all, because they are still raw and squeaking under resistance as you crunch into them.

Once the method and the reasons for taking the various steps have been understood, you will begin to see that recipes are less relevant than the techniques themselves and the kitchen will all of a sudden become a friendly place.

Traditionally, one of the cardinal rules of the kitchen is that green vegetables are always cooked in 'heavily boiling', heavily salted water, the salt 'fixing' the colour in the vegetable. To say 'heavily boiling' is nonsense, however, as water can either boil or not boil. Simmering can certainly have different levels but not boiling; it either is or it isn't.

We were forced to look more closely into the technique of cooking green vegetables at the Fat Duck because our gas pressure was so low that we could barely boil a large pan of water. The only conclusion I could come up with as to what action the salt actually plays was in raising the temperature at which the water boils.

There is an enzyme in green beans that can destroy chlorophyll. The activity of this is more energetic at lower temperatures and is destroyed when the temperature approaches 100°C. This, however, plays only a small role in affecting colour and flavour. On further investigation, it would appear that salt only marginally increases the boiling temperature of water and really not to any degree that will affect the cooking of green vegetables.

Some people use the argument that when you throw a handful of salt into a pan of boiling water it erupts, proving that the salt is increasing the boiling temperature of the water. This eruption is in fact caused by the movement of the salt falling through the water, helping bubbles to form.

Salting the water definitely has little effect on seasoning. At the Fat Duck we were salting the blanching water 80g per litre, which is quite a significant amount. However, when the beans were refreshed, they still needed seasoning.

Without becoming too boringly technical, it is the calcium content of the water that is the vital element here. Hard water, or, to be more precise, water with high levels of calcium in it, will make the vegetables tougher. This means that the beans will take longer to soften, and will turn brown. Softened water, with a neutral or slightly alkaline pH, is ideal, as the chlorophyll retains its green colour. Our water was so 'hard' that we began cooking our green vegetables in bottled water! We now have a unit attached to one of our taps that removes calcium from the water.

One other piece of kitchen folklore is that you must never cook green vegetables with the lid on or they will discolour. One day last year, I was talking with a friend about the cooking of green vegetables (as you do) and he asked me whether I had ever made the experiment comparing cooking green beans with the lid on or off. My initial reaction was, 'Of course I have!' When I paused to think about it, however, I realized that I had never compared the 2 methods side by side.

So we made the test. We took 2 pans of the same size and made from the same material. They were filled with the same quantity of water and the pH in each pan was measured. They were the same. Both pans were placed on the heat and brought to the boil. Some haricot beans bought from the market that morning were prepared in 2 equal quantities.

The beans were simultaneously dropped into the boiling water and a lid was immediately placed on one of the pans. The 2 lots of beans were cooked for the same amount of time until done and then drained and refreshed. These beans were then shown to a couple of testers who were not party to the preparation. No one could tell the difference between the beans cooked in a pan with the lid on or the one with the lid off.

It really is quite amazing that a piece of kitchen lore like this has been in existence for so many years without being questioned, particularly when it is such an easy test to make!

If you are in an experimental frame of mind, why not test another piece of kitchen lore? Plunging green vegetables into iced water to fix the colour – is it really necessary? You may have to compensate a little for the beans that are to be allowed to cool down naturally by taking them out of their boiling water a minute or so earlier than the ones that are to be plunged into the iced water.

It was these studies of green beans that initiated contact with my friend Peter Barham, a physicist at Bristol University. Peter is leading the way in this country in the science of cooking, and we spend many an hour discussing techniques from our different perspectives. I had come to the conclusion that salt was not required in order to keep the green colour in vegetables. Having spoken to Peter, however, although my conclusion was correct, some of my theories for arriving at it were a little misplaced.

Here are my steps to perfectly cooked haricots verts.

1. Take a casserole (not an aluminium pan or the vegetables will discolour) and fill it with water, measuring out 1 litre for every 100g of beans.
2. Top and tail the beans, either using a knife or, preferably, by hand. Hold the bean in one hand and with the thumb and forefinger of the other hand, gently snap off each end of the bean, carefully pulling away so that any vein running down the side comes away with it.

★ Children's tip

Topping and tailing the beans by hand will be a great exercise for the kids, as they will be able to look a little more at the quality of the bean. They should be looking for green beans that are quite flimsy. The more stiff they are, the less fresh the bean will be and the more it will require soaking. Once they have done it a few times, it will be quite a quick process. More importantly, however, they will learn to differentiate between good- and poor-quality vegetables. The older, bigger bean will tend to have a vein that will come away when it is topped and tailed, and the better, younger bean will be less woody and slightly more flexible. A good bean should bend before snapping.

3. Soak the beans in cold water for a couple of hours before cooking. Quite often, these beans will have been picked over a month before being shipped. Soaking will help to rehydrate them.

4. Bring the water to the boil on a high heat, with a lid on.

5. If you have soft water, do not add any salt. If, however, your water is hard, you can either cook the beans in neutral bottled water, which you may find an unnecessary expense, or add a minuscule amount of bicarbonate of soda (this is a little risky, though, as too much and the taste and texture may be ruined).

6. Drain the beans completely and when the water is boiling, plunge them in. Immediately put the lid on and boil until tender – start testing them after 3 minutes but they may take up to 10.

7. Have a bowl of iced or cold water to hand. When the beans are cooked, test by tasting them (they should have a slight resistance but no crunch), drain them through a colander and tip into the cold water. Do not, as some people do, put the pan under the tap – the beans will take too long to cool down. Do not, either, leave the beans under cold, running water or they will lose their flavour.

8. As soon as the beans are cold, drain them and set them aside until you want to use them. You can prepare them a few hours in advance, which can be quite convenient.

9. When you are ready to serve the beans, simply reheat them in a mix of one third unsalted butter to two thirds water (tap water is fine for this stage). Simmer them for a couple of minutes with salt and freshly ground black pepper, drain and serve. Do not reheat the beans in too much of this emulsion;

use approximately 50g of butter and 100ml of water for every 100g of beans.

The method is exactly the same for all other green vegetables: broccoli, lettuce, sugar-snap peas, runner beans, etc. The cooking times may also differ depending on whether or not you wish to reheat the vegetables, serve them immediately or use them in a salad.

Some chopped shallots and chopped fresh herbs such as parsley, chervil or chives would be a nice addition.

Salad of Haricots Verts

As well as being an essential part of salad Niçoise, these beans make their very own delicious salad. Simply mix them with chopped shallots, herbs and some very finely sliced fresh white button mushrooms. Toss in some vinaigrette with mustard added, season with salt and freshly ground black pepper, and serve.

Before using beans in a salad, make sure that they are completely drained of all moisture. This will ensure that they absorb the vinaigrette and seasoning.

Haricots à la Crème

These are a real favourite with all our children. They go brilliantly with any of the lamb or chicken dishes in the Sunday lunch chapter.

Cook the beans by the basic method but stop them cooking a couple of minutes before you would normally do so.

For 200g of haricot beans, peel and very finely slice 10 shallots and crush 1/2 a clove of garlic. Sweat these in 75g of unsalted butter on a low heat for about 10 minutes, until the shallots are translucent and the garlic has lost its aggressive aroma.

Add the cold beans, 50g more butter in cubes, 50ml of whipping or double cream and 75ml of water. Season very generously with salt and freshly ground black pepper and cook on a high heat for 3–4 minutes until the liquid has a sauce-like consistency.

Stir in a good heaped teaspoon of grain mustard, season again if necessary, and sprinkle over a good tablespoon of chopped fresh parsley. Make sure you add the mustard at the last minute: if they are cooked for too long with the mustard, the beans will turn an unappetizing yellowy-brown colour.

Asparagus

One of the few vegetables that we can truly say is best British is asparagus, but unfortunately, it is around for such a short time each year. So, how should we make the most of this vegetable while we have it?

Asparagus does not benefit from being blanched, refreshed and reheated. Far from it – it actually loses much of its flavour. You only need to taste the water in which the asparagus has been cooked to realize how much flavour is lost from the vegetable itself.

The best way to cook asparagus is first to peel it, using a small knife if necessary. Put it into a frying pan with a generous amount of butter, and cook on a low to medium heat. It may be necessary to add a little water in order to stop the butter from colouring. The asparagus should take approximately 8 minutes to cook for medium to large spears. You will be amazed at just how intense the flavour and colour are.

Asparagus has a wonderful affinity with shallots, mushrooms and, above all, chervil. Start off with some finely chopped shallots in the pan with the butter and, after about 5 minutes of gentle cooking, add the asparagus and a few very finely sliced button mushrooms. A few drops of water will create a delicious sauce. Finish by scattering over a generous amount of chopped chervil; delicious.

Braised Lettuces

These are a delicious accompaniment to meat dishes, particularly pot-roast pork (page 153) or roast chicken (page 158), and are easy to prepare.

Put the butter into a small pan and place on a medium heat. It will begin to bubble and turn brown. When the sizzling noise starts to die down, the butter will become darker and take on a nutty aroma. When this happens, skim off any foam that has risen to the surface, strain the butter through a fine sieve or tea strainer into a bowl and set aside. (This is known as beurre noisette, as it develops a nutty aroma when cooking. 'Noisette' is French for hazelnut.)

Serves 4 as a garnish
100g unsalted butter
2 Cos (Romaine) lettuces
150ml chicken stock or water
salt and freshly ground black pepper

Prepare the lettuces by removing the outer leaves, say 4 in total, as they tend to be a bit on the tough side, and cut each head of lettuce in half, lengthways. With the inside of the lettuce facing you, pull out and snap off the very small, yellow inner leaves, definitely something for the children to do. (Keep these leaves – they'll make a delicious salad.) With a small knife, cut out, in a V shape, the root of the lettuce. Wash the lettuces and pat them dry.

Blanch the lettuces following the method described above for green beans (page 202). Cook them in boiling water for about 4 minutes, then drain and refresh. As soon as they are cold, remove them from the water and gently squeeze the excess liquid out of them. In a saucepan big enough to hold the lettuces in one layer, place them side by side without overlapping. Pour over the butter and the chicken stock or water. Bring the liquid to a gentle boil, and as soon as it boils, reduce the heat to a simmer.

Place a cartouche (see page 50) on top and cook at a gentle simmer for about 10 minutes. The aim is to have the lettuces soft but with a very slight bite, and still retaining some of their nice green colour. Drain and gently pat them dry. Season with salt and pepper before serving.

As well as Cos lettuce, Little Gem works well. Even pak choi is delicious cooked this way. Also, try the recipe using celery. You will need to use celery hearts, which are available from most supermarkets. Just peel them by lightly running a peeler vertically along their length. Do not be too fanatical about removing all of the strings – you do not want to penetrate the flesh too much. Halve the celery hearts, cut out the root as with the lettuce, and follow the same braising method, allowing an extra 20 minutes cooking time.

★ Tip
You should try this recipe – you will be surprised, especially if you are not over-keen on celery. Many people dismiss this vegetable and use it mainly for stews or soups, discarding or blending it before serving. If you are not a celery lover, the chances are that you will not be the first in line to give it to your children. Hopefully, this method will change all of that.

It is important that, as parents, we do not allow our own personal likes and dislikes to be passed on to our children. They should be allowed to decide for themselves whether they like something or not. Remember also that what they like or dislike today may well turn out to be the opposite in the future.

★ Children's tip

Chefs spend many hours each day in the kitchen and, without really thinking about it, develop subconscious awareness. An example of this, one that would be a great thing to teach your children, is sound! What am I talking about? Well, to give you an example, take the nutty butter (beurre noisette) that was prepared for the lettuces. While the butter is cooking, it will sizzle. As it begins to turn brown and the water content disappears, the sizzling will die down. When there is no noise coming from the pan, the butter will start to burn. This means that when you have done this once or twice, you and your children will be able to busy yourselves in the kitchen, knowing that when there is no longer any sound, the butter is turning brown!

Carrots

Here are two carrot recipes. In some ways, the second recipe is a progression from the first. They are both equally good. The first recipe is simpler and concentrates just on the taste of the carrot. Where children are concerned, it is probably best to 'wean them' on this dish first, before progressing to the next.

★ Children's tip
We found that peeling carrots was one of the first kitchen tasks that our children enjoyed doing. Each time we prepared Sunday lunch, our oldest two would demand carrots. At first we thought that it was great that at the ages of four and six our children were already enjoying vegetables. We soon realized that it was not that they loved carrots so much but that they enjoyed peeling them. Strangely enough, however, it was not long before they began to like the taste of the end result. It just goes to show that perseverance can pay off. These recipes can be carried out entirely by your children, including all the measuring if they are old enough.

Root vegetables like carrots and potatoes should be stored out of the fridge in a dark place; if stored in a cold environment the starches convert to sugars, which is not desirable. Otherwise, vegetables in general require high humidity or they will lose moisture from their cell walls and become limp.

Tomatoes, on the other hand, must not be stored in the fridge or they will lose most of their flavour. To see the effect of this, get your children to test tomatoes of the same ripeness and preferably from the same vine. Store a couple in the fridge and leave a couple out of the fridge. After a week, taste-test them.

The general quality of carrots available in this country is quite shocking. They may look perfectly formed, orange and shiny, but they have almost no flavour. We were in France last year on holiday and the local greengrocer had some carrots for sale. I was drawn to these by the fact that they were absolutely caked in earth. I picked one up and was surprised to feel that the carrot was, in fact, quite soft. Expecting to smell just the earth, I could not have been more wrong: it was the sweetest, most intense-smelling carrot I had ever come across. I bought some and we ate them that night with a thick veal chop, cooked over vines. They were quite amazing. It highlighted the substandard quality of the vegetables that we in the UK are supplied with.

Glazed Carrots

A lot of the flavour molecules in carrots are water-soluble. This effectively means that the carrots will lose flavour to the water that they are cooked in. To get around this, they are cooked in butter with a lid on. The steam produced will be sufficient moisture to stop them from burning. If you are worried about timing the cooking of these carrots to go with the rest of the meal, they can be done in advance and gently reheated on the top of the stove or in the oven.

First, top, tail and peel the carrots. Cut them into discs; this can be done across the carrot so that they are completely round, or diagonally so that they have a more elongated shape. It's not important, merely aesthetic. You need to make sure that they are all the same thickness – about 2cm. This ensures that the carrots will be cooked evenly.

Serves 4 as an accompaniment
8 nice, bright, medium-sized carrots
75g butter
1 teaspoon icing sugar
salt and freshly ground black pepper

Now take a casserole or frying pan with a lid, preferably large enough to fit the carrots side by side without them being on top of each other. Add the butter and icing sugar to the pan, season with salt and pepper and put the lid on.

Place the pan on a low heat and let the carrots cook very gently. From time to time, shake the pan. The first time you do this you will need to take a little care in case your heat source is too powerful. If it looks as if the butter is getting too hot and the carrots may start to fry, add a dessertspoon of water and put the lid back on. The carrots will become beautifully glazed. Season again and serve.

As an alternative, the carrots can be cooked a little longer until they begin to brown.

Carrots Glazed with Cumin and Orange

This is essentially a variation on the previous recipe, involving ingredients that bring both a Provençal and an oriental note to the dish.

This recipe uses orange zest only. The acids in orange juice interfere with the cooking of the carrot. The same problem will occur with potatoes.

Like the previous recipe, these carrots can be cooked in advance and reheated.

Serves 2 as a main garnish or 4 as an accompaniment

500g carrots

1 clove of garlic

5g cumin seeds

6 cardamom seeds, removed from their pods (1–2 pods should yield this amount)

8 sprigs of fresh thyme

3 soupspoons olive oil

75g unsalted butter

10g sugar (this amount will vary slightly, depending on the quality of the carrots)

zest of 1 orange, removed with a peeler, taking care to leave as much of the white pith behind as possible

salt and freshly ground black pepper

Peel the carrots and slice them diagonally into 1cm thick rounds. Peel and crush the garlic.

Heat a small frying pan until hot without adding any oil, and put in the cumin and cardamom seeds. Toast these for a few minutes until they begin to release their oils (you will be able to smell them). Tie the thyme sprigs together with string.

Take a pan large enough to hold the carrots in one layer if possible (but not too large). Put in the carrots, garlic, spices, thyme, olive oil and butter, place the pan over a low to medium heat, and sweat the carrots for 5 minutes. Add the sugar and cook for a few minutes more. Add a few drops of water just to cool the carrots down a little, then add the orange zest and place a lid on the pan. Continue cooking until the carrots are tender.

Once the carrots are cooked, remove the lid and if there is any moisture left in the pan, reduce it until the carrots are nice and slippery. Season and serve.

Pommes Purée or Mashed Potato

These two potato recipes may seem lengthy but the results will be well worth it. They also have the added benefit that they can be made in advance and will keep for a few days in the fridge, needing only a little last-minute preparation. These two potato dishes seem to form the staple of many a child's dinner, so why not let them get involved in making them?

The first describes a purée that is silkily smooth and enriched, sometimes greatly, with good butter; the second a good old-fashioned mash, made with a masher or even crushed with a fork. This latter method seems to have become very trendy in recent years.

The important thing here is the basic principle of the first cooking or, almost, soaking of the potatoes. I discovered this principle from the book *The Man Who Ate Everything* by Jeffrey Steingarten, who devotes a chapter to puréed potatoes. The producers of dried potato flakes and powdered mashed potato have spent considerable sums of money in trying to avoid gelatinous or starchy potatoes, which render the purée elastic.

The method that Jeffrey Steingarten describes interested me when I read it, as we were at the time trying many variations and techniques to improve our potato purée at the Fat Duck.

Without becoming too technical and before your eyes begin to glaze over completely, this method basically involves pre-cooking the potatoes at a temperature where the starch begins to gelatinize, cooling them down, and then cooking them in hotter water, allowing the individual cells to separate from one another. This makes it possible to mash the potatoes without any free starch leaking out of them. Along with a couple of other careful steps, you will end up with a glue-free purée.

The beauty with this is that, first, the purée is better, and second, all you have to do is make a batch up and keep it in the fridge. When you want to use it, just reheat it in a pan, gradually adding simmering milk while whisking; it takes about 3 minutes. It is because of the emulsified starch that you can do this.

For this recipe, use the best possible quality unsalted butter that you can get your hands on.

When we first opened the Fat Duck, I was trying to discover the best potatoes that were available at that time for puréeing. I had read that to find the most appropriate potato for the job in hand, you first need to determine whether or not it is waxy or mealy. I prefer using waxy potatoes for mash, as they tend to produce a more creamy result, although if you are not careful they may result in a purée that is a little starchier.

★ Children's tip

Make a saline solution of 1 part salt to 11 parts water. If, when a potato is plopped in this, it floats, it will be waxy and if it sinks, mealy. With this valuable information to hand, my wife journeyed around the main local supermarkets with the kids and her trusty container of salted water. She was greeted with mixed reactions from the different supermarkets, ranging from helpful to 'Call the police!'

The choice of potato can be a bit of a minefield. As a general rule, most of the red varieties make a decent purée, and if you

can find them, large Belle de Fontenay or Charlotte potatoes give you a good end result.

For 4 people, take 1kg of potatoes, peel them and cut them into slices about 2.5cm thick. The important thing here is to make sure that the potatoes are exactly the same thickness, as a difference of only a few millimetres could mean ending up with cooked and uncooked potatoes at the same time, which for me is the main problem with cooking them whole, in their skins. Run these slices under the cold tap to wash off any starch on the surface of the potato.

Heat a pan of water, enough to cover the potatoes completely, to 175° Fahrenheit. Add the potatoes and maintain the temperature at 160°F for half an hour. Holding the temperature of the water in this range may seem like a bit of a nightmare, but after the first attempt, you will find the appropriate setting to keep a given quantity of water in the required temperature range. For example, if your heat supply is not low enough to keep the temperature down to 160°F with the potatoes in, then you will need to increase the volume of water.

★ **Tip**
This method will be easier to follow using a thermometer graduated in Fahrenheit. The reason for this is that there is a narrow margin for error when precooking the potatoes. A thermometer graduated in Fahrenheit will give a 10° margin while one graduated in Centigrade has only a couple of degrees to play with.

The slices will become opaque and tough. Have ready a bowl of iced water. When the potatoes are at this stage, drain them and plump them into the iced water. Leave them in it until completely cold, then drain them. Rinse the pan out and fill it to the same level as before. Salt the water as you would do normally and bring it to the boil. Drop in the potatoes and cook them in simmering water until soft; with this method, they will probably take longer than you might expect. Just be patient.

When done, drain the potatoes and dry them out a little. This can be done by putting the potatoes in a pan on a low heat and gently shaking them.

The potatoes can now be used in one of the three following recipes.

1. Good Old-fashioned Mash

Simply add butter, olive oil or a combination of both, and some simmering milk, cream or a mix of the two, and mash the potatoes as normal. If the mash is not to be used immediately, simply add the butter as above and allow the mix to cool down before putting it in an airtight container in the fridge.

When ready to serve, just heat it gently in a pan, whisking in a little of the hot milk or cream to taste.

2. Crushed Potatoes

With a fork, crush the potatoes while adding butter and/ or olive oil along with your choice of other ingredients. You can add chopped shallots, confit tomatoes (see page 57), chopped herbs such as parsley, chives, chervil, basil or coriander, olives or capers, bacon . . . the list is almost endless.

Try to end up with mashed potato that still has small morsels of potato in it to give a variation in texture.

If this is not to be eaten immediately, cool and refrigerate without adding the flavourings. Just reheat the potatoes in the oven before adding them.

3. Pommes Purée

At the restaurant, this dish is made with just milk and butter – quite large quantities of butter. You can add up to 400g of unsalted butter for every kilo of potatoes! If making this purée mainly as a source of meals for the children, use less butter – say 200g per kg of potato. If, however, the purée is for a big lunch or a special dinner, increase the quantity of butter to 300g.

A potato ricer is ideal, although a vegetable mill should also do the job. Have ready a bowl with the cold butter in it, cut into cubes of about 2.5cm. With the cooked potatoes still hot, push them through the ricer on to the cubed butter. Never use a food processor to purée the potatoes unless you want to end up with savoury bubblegum! At the Fat Duck, a flat, very fine-meshed drum sieve is used to pass the purée with the butter through a second time, giving it a light and silky texture.

Once again, the purée can be prepared in advance up to this stage. It will keep in the fridge for a few days. To serve, just reheat it gently in a pan while gradually whisking in a little simmering milk.

Some melted cheese, chopped herbs or grain mustard would make a welcome addition to the purée.

Gratin of Potatoes

Our children love this: creamy, meltingly soft potatoes with a delicate sweet taste of garlic.

There are several secrets to it. The potatoes are simmered in the flavoured milk before baking in order to extract some of the starch. This enables a creamy texture to be achieved while keeping the dish light; the starch-thickened liquid means that less cream needs to be added. Slicing the potatoes thinly means that there is more surface area of potato and more flavour. Finally, a good gratin should be cooked for a long period of time at a low temperature. This will leave the potatoes as soft as butter while holding their shape, and the sauce will be completely integrated.

You will need a baking dish at least 5cm deep and measuring about 25 × 15cm.

Serves 6

400ml whole milk (enough to just cover the potatoes in the pan: adjust accordingly)

3 fresh bay leaves (optional)

1 bunch of fresh thyme (optional)

1 clove of garlic, crushed, or 2 teaspoons of confit garlic purée (page 196)

1kg potatoes, washed (red potatoes such as Desirée or Romano are good for this)

200ml double cream

75g unsalted butter

salt and cayenne pepper

nutmeg

Preheat the oven to 120°C/gas mark ½.

Pour the milk into a saucepan and add the herbs and crushed garlic or garlic purée. On a medium heat, bring the milk to the boil and leave to simmer for 5 minutes. Remove from the heat and leave to cool so that the milk infuses with the herbs and garlic. Once infused, strain to remove the herbs. If the herbs are not being used, simply combine the milk and garlic in the pan and set aside.

Peel the potatoes and slice them as thinly as possible. Use a mandolin if available, alternatively slice the potatoes with a knife – but just watch the fingers! The potatoes should be 1–2mm thick.

Add the sliced potatoes to the milk, separating them as much as possible, and place the pan on a medium heat. Bring the liquid to a simmer, stirring occasionally to stop them from sticking. Try to keep the potatoes separated as much as possible. After a few minutes, the milk will have thickened with the starch from the potatoes. When this happens, add the cream and butter and gently agitate the pan so that everything is mixed in.

Finally, add the salt, cayenne pepper and nutmeg. Be careful – cayenne pepper is strong stuff. This gratin will take more salt than expected, as the potatoes absorb quite a lot, leaving the gratin less seasoned once cooked.

Pour the potatoes into the oven dish, trying to get them as flat as possible. A perforated slice is ideal for pressing them down. The potatoes should be covered by about 0.5cm of liquid. A little less is fine, but if there is more, do not add it. Tightly cover the dish with tin foil and bake in the oven for 4 hours. Every 45 minutes or so, gently press down on the potatoes with the back of a slice.

Just before serving, flash the dish under the grill to gratinate it.

This dish actually improves when made in advance and reheated. Place a weighted dish on top of the gratin dish (with the foil still on) when slightly cooled. The potatoes will absorb any excess liquid overnight. To reheat, put in a low oven until warmed through and then finish under the grill. When reheating this dish, it is important to remember that you must do so on a low temperature, otherwise it will split and become grainy. 110°C/gas mark ¼ for 20 minutes should be fine.

★ Children's tip
Depending on the kids' tastes, some cheese could be added: use Parmesan or Cheddar, or experiment with some of the more unusual cheeses now available. It's a good way to introduce children to cheeses that they might not otherwise want to try. Grate the cheese and sprinkle it between the layers of potato.

★ Variation
There are, as usual, many variations; for example, some grated horse-radish or grain mustard could be added to the milk. However, please try grating a little lime zest over the gratin – it really is wonderful.

This dish can be turned into a main meal by adding bacon and serving it with a fried egg.

Chips

The French in their gastronomic wisdom do not just have chips. Oh no, they have several versions, relating basically to their size:

- Pommes paille (straw potatoes): the potatoes are cut into 7–8cm lengths the thickness of matchsticks.
- Pommes allumettes (matchstick potatoes): these are cut to a thickness of about 0.5cm.
- Pommes Pont-Neuf: the potatoes are cut to about 1cm or a little thicker. They are named after a bridge in Paris, supposedly slightly curving the way the bridge does! These are my preferred chips, as this thickness yields a really crunchy exterior while keeping the interior light and fluffy.

As with many potato dishes, the variety of potato itself is very important. At the Fat Duck Golden Wonder potatoes, grown for us by an excellent farmer not far from Newbury, are used. For home use, try Charlotte or Belle de Fontenay.

Many hours spent experimenting with various methods of chip-making have come up with the following recipe. It may seem rather lengthy but it does produce the best chips that I have ever tasted. With the right variety of potato, these chips are crispy on the outside and light and fluffy on the inside, retaining their crunch for almost 10 minutes after they have been cooked.

The beauty of this method is that the potatoes can be cooked twice and kept in the fridge until required. They will keep like this for at least 1 week. To serve, simply plunge them into hot oil until crisp.

★ Variation

The traditional double cooking method of making chips works fine, but they are, however, just not the same. Try the comparison for yourself.

A couple of years ago, one of the top chefs in Paris used a technique for cooking chips one time only. He simply started them off in warm oil and gradually increased the temperature. The benefit of this is that the chips absorb less fat. Here's why. Imagine the chip as it heats up. Steam will build up in the centre, where there is a mass of soft potato. This steam will be creating an outward pressure, which will in turn prevent any fat from being absorbed. Traditionally, when the chip is removed from the cooler oil at the end of the first cooking process, hot oil will be on the surface of the chip. As the chip cools down, the steam will disappear and with it the outward pressure, allowing some of the oil to be absorbed. Therefore, by starting the chip off in warm oil and gradually increasing the temperature, the outward pressure created by the steam will prevent the chips from soaking up much oil. This oil can be largely absorbed by paper when draining them.

Give this a whirl, although in terms of a light and fluffy chip with a crisp outside that stays crisp for quite a while after cooking, my method has no equal! The steam created from the inside the chip is also the reason why it loses its crisp coating.

At the Fat Duck, various methods were worked on to reduce some of the moisture inside the chip after the first water blanching. They were dried in the oven but this just made the chip too tough, as did the precooking method used for the pommes purée recipe (page 216). We even tried making pinpricks along the sides of the chip while still hot, but obviously this was completely impractical! We now use a bowl with a valve on the side of it called a desiccator. It has a pump attached to it. The chips are put in this immediately after coming out of the blanching water. The pump then pulls a vacuum on them! This extracts the moisture and cools them down. This process is repeated after the second cooking (the first oil blanching). Obviously this is not to suggest that you do this at home, but it does work brilliantly.

In terms of which cooking fat to use, groundnut oil is probably the best, as it is very clean and odour-free. If you want to be really adventurous, use fat that you have rendered yourself. At the restaurant, veal kidney fat is used, rendered by roasting in the oven until golden, strained off. This is used for the final cooking of the chips. Beef, goose or duck fat would also be delicious. Not the most healthy alternative but a real treat for an occasional dinner.

★ **Children's tip**

It may seem like a bit of a waste of time washing potatoes when the skin will be discarded anyway, but, believe me, if your kids are going to try their hand at cutting a potato into chips, you will want a clean potato to start with. Otherwise any earth will transfer itself to the chopping board, hands, clothes, floor . . . the list is endless!

Serves 4

1.2kg potatoes

1 litre groundnut oil

1 litre rendered fat (optional – if you do not wish to use this, 1 litre of groundnut oil will be sufficient for both the first and second frying processes)

Wash the potatoes. With a sharp kitchen knife, square them into rectangles and then cut them into chips about 1cm thick. The length of the chips is not so important, but try to keep them the same thickness so that they will cook at the same rate. You can use the trimmings for sautéing with, for example, some onions and bacon. This would make a delicious dinner with, perhaps, a fried egg.

As soon as the chips are cut, put them into a bowl under cold running water for 10 minutes or so to rinse off some of the starch, then drain them.

Next, bring a casserole of unsalted water to the boil and plunge in the drained potatoes. Bring back to the boil and simmer gently until the point of a knife will penetrate the chips easily. It is important to make sure that the water is only just simmering. If it boils too aggressively the potatoes will begin to break up before they are cooked sufficiently.

Very carefully lift the potatoes out of the water, using a slotted spoon, and place them on a tray. Allow them to steam cool, then place them in the fridge. The chips will harden when cold.

For the next stage, heat the groundnut oil to a temperature of 130°C and plunge in the chips. After a while, they will take on a drier appearance (do not let them brown at all). When this happens, they have finished their second cooking process; drain them, let them cool to room temperature, and put them into the fridge. When cold, they are ready for their final cooking.

If using rendered fat for this, heat it to 180°C. Alternatively, use groundnut oil. Plunge in the chips and cook until golden brown. This may take 8–10 minutes; be patient in order to obtain a really crisp chip.

Drain and season with salt only; they will take quite a lot.

With these chips and the baked beans, fried egg and tomato ketchup recipes, the kids could have the junior version of haut gastronomy!

Remember, if time does not allow these chips to be cooked from start to finish in one go, they can be made over a day or so, and stored in the fridge between each process.

Roast Potatoes

These must be just about the most adored traditional English vegetable dish. It is definitely one of the best smells that fills our house on a Sunday. There are almost never enough of them.

As well as using the right potato, it is important never to salt the cooking water, otherwise the potatoes will not crisp up well. Make sure that, as with the chips, the potatoes are cooked for as long as possible in very gently simmering water.

Some people grill their potatoes, which does obtain a crunchy result; they are, however, just not the same. And it is quite common practice, especially in some pubs – shock-horror! – to finish the roast potatoes off in the deep-fat fryer!

My children adore these, and have been peeling the potatoes for the Sunday lunch for a few years now.

If, when you coat the potatoes with the flour, they break up a bit, do not worry; these broken pieces are absolutely delicious, as they become really crunchy.

Preheat the oven to 180°C/gas mark 4.

Wash and peel the potatoes. Cut them in half or into three, depending on their size, and leave them in a bowl under water for 5–10 minutes.

Bring a pan of unsalted water to the boil and plunge in the potatoes. Cook until they are soft, not quite as long as for the

Serves 4

1kg potatoes (same varieties as for chips – see page 225)

olive oil (enough to fill whatever roasting tray you use to a depth of just under 1cm)

1 tablespoon plain flour

4 cloves of garlic

1 generous bunch of fresh rosemary

1 bunch of fresh thyme

salt

chips (see page 225), as you will be lightly tossing them in flour and do not want them to break up.

Meanwhile, pour the olive oil into a roasting tray large enough to hold all the potatoes in one layer. The oil should be just under 1cm in depth. Put the tray into the preheated oven.

When the potatoes are done, drain them in a colander and sieve the flour over them. Carefully turn them in the flour so that they do not break up, and place them in the roasting tray, together with the cloves of garlic. Turn the potatoes in the oil and put the tray into the oven. They should take about 1½ hours. If possible, turn the potatoes every 20 minutes. After half an hour, add the herbs.

Drain the potatoes when golden brown, season with salt and serve. Your patience will be rewarded!

Baked Potatoes

It is not really possible to leave this recipe out, as it is such a simple foundation for a meal. With only a few guidelines, you should be able to have wonderfully crispy baked potatoes every time.

Simply make sure that the potato is oiled. The oil keeps the temperature of the potato skin high and, as potatoes lose moisture while baking, an un-oiled potato will be more likely to be softened both by this loss of moisture and by the fact that the skin will not remain as hot during baking.

Cook in a very hot oven for an hour or so.

When cooked, the flesh can be scooped out into a bowl and crushed with a fork. There is a whole range of other ingredients that can be added: ratatouille, potted mackerel, shredded oxtail, lamb leftovers mixed with a little goat's cheese . . . Filled again, the potatoes have become a complete meal.

Pea Purée

Nearly all fruits and vegetables begin to deteriorate once picked. It is a very sad fact, but fresh peas, bought in season from the supermarket, will have little taste. By the time that they have been put on the supermarket shelves, they will be at least a few days old.

If you are lucky enough to grow your own peas or have access to peas that have been picked within the last day, then they will be fantastic. Unfortunately, most of us do not have that opportunity. All is, however, not lost. Without sounding like a walking advertisement for them, Bird's Eye have recognized this fact and they freeze the pea within hours of it being picked, preserving its sweetness.

★ **Children's tip**

This recipe could not be simpler. It's great for children – they can easily prepare the whole dish from start to finish and they will definitely not get bored, as the purée can be made in 5 minutes. This purée is great as an accompaniment to almost anything and can also be stirred into risottos or pasta dishes. I loved buttered pea sandwiches as a child; you really should try them!

There is a minimum quantity with which this purée can be made. If, too little, it will not purée sufficiently in the blender.

Defrost the peas under cold running water or in the micro-wave. Take care not to cook them at all.

Serves 4

400g Bird's Eye frozen peas (preferably not petits pois, as these have too much skin to flesh and will tend to make the purée more granular)

75g unsalted butter

salt and freshly ground black pepper

Reduce them to a purée in the liquidizer, making sure it is left running for 5 minutes on full power. Please note that a food processor will not do this job particularly well.

Pass the peas through the finest-meshed sieve available.

Put the purée into a small pan and gently heat it, adding the butter.

Do not heat the purée up too much or for too long, other-wise it will become lumpy and lose its wonderful colour. Season to taste – it needs a lot of salt and pepper.

The purée will keep in the fridge for a couple of days in its raw state. Cover it with clingfilm, making sure that the cling-film comes into contact with the surface of the purée to stop it losing its colour. Simply reheat it as required, adding the butter and seasoning.

Buttered Cabbage

This simple recipe is delicious and very versatile. Our children love cabbage prepared this way. Perhaps the butter has something to do with it!

Discard the outer leaves of the cabbage, as they will be tough. Remove all the remaining leaves and wash them. Now cut each leaf in half, discarding the central, tough vein.

Put the cabbage into a casserole with the butter. Place on a medium heat with the lid on. Shake the pan regularly – the build-up of heat will cause steam, which will help to cook the cabbage. After approximately 5 minutes, remove the lid and continue cooking until done.

Season and serve.

Serves 4

2 green or Savoy cabbages

60g unsalted butter, cut into 5 pieces

salt and freshly ground black pepper

Dried Cabbage Leaves

This is an unusual way of dealing with cabbage.

Set the oven to about 70°C/gas mark ⅛ or lower.

Make a simple sugar syrup using 100ml of water and 100g of caster sugar. Bring the water and sugar to the boil and, while stirring, remove from the heat as soon as the sugar has dissolved. Leave to cool.

Remove and discard the outer leaves from a Savoy cabbage. Take off 8 of the remaining leaves from the cabbage and cook them in boiling salted water for 8–10 minutes (see the method for the haricots verts on page 202). Drain, refresh and lightly pat the leaves dry on a tea towel. If necessary, leave them to dry in a warm ventilated place; as far as possible try to minimize any moisture remaining on the leaves.

With a brush, coat the leaves in the sugar syrup and put them into the oven to dry. This will probably take about 1 hour, although it may take a little longer, depending on the cabbage. Brush the leaves with more syrup once or twice while they are drying.

Remove from the oven when they are dry and allow them to crisp up as they cool. They should become shiny and crisp.

★ **Children's tip**
This recipe is a great little experiment for the children to do. It's a useful exercise in dispelling any preconceived ideas that we might have

about what we expect foods to taste of and which part of the meal they should be used for.

This recipe is in this chapter rather than the dessert section as it is designed to show your children that what we expect to be sweet isn't always so. After all, vanilla is a savoury spice. It is just that we always associate it with sweet dishes. Try this mainly as an experiment and try to imagine what the leaves would go well with. Poached pears or peaches would be good.

Braised Lentils

It was quite a challenge to get our children to enjoy lentils. Cooked properly, they are delicious. They are, however, an adult taste and one that you can learn to enjoy as you grow up. As children tend to love making soups we found that introducing them to lentil soup was the best way forward. This worked well and now they enjoy lentils with, for example, sausages and pommes purée.

Lentils have many nutritional attributes as a vegetable, being the second best source of vegetable protein after soya, and a very high source of good carbohydrate. We never ate lentils as children; mainly because they were not really available then. You can now buy red lentils, green lentils and Puy lentils, which are generally regarded as the best ones readily available in the shops.

★ **Tip**
The lentil comes from the pod of a small annual plant originally grown in Egypt. The Puy lentil from France has become a gourmet vegetable. Many lentils, however, are now cultivated in Canada. At the Fat Duck a slate-green lentil called the Castellucio, which comes from Italy, is the preferred choice.

Instead of soaking lentils prior to cooking, they are just brought to the boil in water, refreshed and returned to the pan to cook slowly with aromatics. The important thing here is to watch the calcium level in the cooking water. If too high, the pulses will harden and split. If using hard water, the lentils should be cooked in bottled water with a low calcium content. A litre bottle of water should be sufficient to blanch and cook enough lentils for 4 people.

The aromatics used in the braising of the lentils are not set in stone: use mainly what is to hand and, to a certain extent, the more the better. Other vegetables can be added, such as fennel, celeriac or celery leaves. The addition of fresh ginger or pineapple will make the lentils much softer, as both these ingredients contain protein-denaturing enzymes and lentils are a relatively high source of protein.

★ Children's tip

I think I should say a few words about preparing vegetables. It is a very important thing to teach children, as it will enable them to think more for themselves in the kitchen. This will ultimately lead to them having greater confidence in what they are doing, as they will understand the reasons for it. The kitchen will then become an even more enjoyable place.

When preparing vegetables, it is always important to think about what they will be used for. For example, the potatoes for the gratin (page 222) needed to be sliced as thinly as possible so that the maximum surface area was exposed in order to extract the starch from the potato to thicken it.

Always try to get your children to think about the vegetable just before they prepare it; get them to hold it in their hand, turn it and consider whether they will be wanting to remove it from the cooking liquid before serving the dish, in which case it should be cut so that it can be easily removed; whether it will be cooked for a relatively short space of time, in which case it should be cut into the smallest pieces possible; whether it needs to be cooked evenly, therefore needing to be cut into uniform, symmetrical pieces.

In the following dish, for example, the vegetables need to be removed, so the carrots are cut lengthways, the onion is left with its root on so that it does not fall apart, the leek is cut across its length and the bouquet garni is tied up. Many recipes will tell you to tie up your herbs; you need only bother to do this if you will be removing them before the end of cooking. If you will be passing everything through a sieve at the end of cooking, there is no need to tie the herbs up.

For this recipe, use bottled mineral water with a low calcium content, as calcium will harden the skins of the lentils and prevent them from cooking properly. Use this water for both the blanching and the cooking of the lentils. Many recipes advise adding salt to dried pulses only towards the end of the cooking time. As mentioned on page 74, this is not necessary; the salt can be added at the beginning as long as the pulses are to have a long, gentle cooking time.

Wash all the vegetables. Top and tail the carrot, peel it and cut it lengthways into quarters. Peel the onion and, keeping the root on, cut it in half. Trim the celery and cut each stick into three pieces. Bash the garlic. Cut off and discard the dark green part of the leek, and cut the rest of it across into 3 equal lengths.

Tie up the herbs.

Put the lentils into a casserole and pour over just enough water to cover them. Bring them to the boil and immediately

Enjoying a snack together

Smooth dark Valrhona chocolate – the best to use for cooking

Chocolate Fondant – p297

Strawberry Soup – p293

Mrs Blumenthal's Cheesecake – p326

Jack making his Raspberry Crunch

Jack's Raspberry Crunch – p328

Enjoying time in the kitchen with my children

Serves 4
1 carrot
1 onion
2 sticks of celery
2 cloves of garlic
1 large leek
a bouquet garni, consisting of fresh thyme, rosemary, bay and parsley
200g Puy lentils
5 rashers of streaky, smoked bacon
75g fresh ginger or pineapple, peeled and sliced
salt and freshly ground black pepper

tip them into a sieve. Rinse the lentils under the tap and return them to the pan. Cover with fresh water so that there is approximately twice the depth of water to lentils.

Add all of the other ingredients and bring to the boil.

Turn down the heat and cook the lentils at a bare simmer (the odd bubble rising to the surface) for at least 1 hour or until tender. They could also be cooked with the lid on in the oven at 100°C/gas mark ¼. Just make sure that they are always covered with water. In the oven, they will take up to 2 hours to cook, though this will vary greatly depending on the quality of the lentils themselves. The lentils should be soft but still whole.

When the lentils are cooked, remove them from the heat and allow them to cool down in the cooking liquid, with the lid on. If you drain them while they are still warm they will dry out and may crack.

The lentils can be kept, covered with a little water, in the fridge for a few days. To serve them plain, simply reheat them in a little of the reserved cooking liquid, as long as it is not too salty, along with a couple of knobs of butter; season with salt and pepper and serve.

Just about anything you want can be added to these. At the Fat Duck, they are served with minced preserved ginger, very finely chopped carrots and leeks and some cubed cucumber. Butter and balsamic vinegar are mixed in at the end.

Some caramelized onions, or any left-over roasting juices that you might have, could be mixed in.

A little sesame oil soy sauce and vinaigrette stirred into the lentils while still warm makes a delicious accompaniment to sausages or ham.

Our children sometimes have them for dinner, with a grilled sausage or some bacon and a soft-boiled egg on top.

Lentil Purée

This works well as an alternative to pommes purée.

Simply take the cooked, drained lentils and either pass them through the finest grille of the mouli or liquidize them with a little of the cooking liquid. Then pass them through the finest-meshed sieve available into a pan.

On a low heat whisk in some unsalted butter and a little cream to taste. Check for seasoning and serve.

Ratatouille

This is a relatively long recipe, but it is just about the best ratatouille recipe around. It will go with almost anything; even in sandwiches, although there are easier sandwich fillings!

★ **Children's tip**

All the work does pay off. It is a great exercise in demonstrating to children one of the points mentioned earlier: the size of the vegetables greatly affects the end result of the dish. Here they are cut uniformly so that they all cook evenly and at the same rate. Also, by cutting them so small, the surface area is massively increased, giving much more flavour to the end result. It also means that in each mouthful many more flavours are perceived at the same time.

Don't be put off by the length of this recipe; it really is worth the effort. It is also a great exercise in knife craft if the kids are old enough, demonstrating the benefit of cutting small and to the same size. It is quite therapeutic, honestly!

This also gives an indication of what lengths some restaurants go to; you never know, it might turn your children into chefs, or put them off for life!

This recipe uses only the outside of the aubergine. The pulp can be used to make a great purée: sweat some onions and garlic in olive oil, and add the aubergine pulp, some fresh thyme leaves and coriander seeds. Cook for about 10–15 minutes, add a generous quantity of fresh basil leaves and purée in a blender.

This can be served hot or cold. A similar purée flavoured with cumin could be made and mixed with some left-over lamb. Simply top with some mashed potato and bake.

Top and tail the aubergines and the courgettes. Take an aubergine and, standing it upright, slice down each edge of the vegetable, removing the skin and about 3mm of flesh, no more. Do the same to all the aubergines and the courgettes.

Use the centres for other purposes such as puréeing, risottos or roasting.

You will now be left with slices of aubergine and courgette. Making sure they are kept separate, as they will not be cooked together, trim the edges off each slice so that you are left with a rectangular shape. Cut each one into strips about 3mm thick, then bunch together the strips and cut across, leaving you with 3mm cubes. Set aside the courgettes. Put the aubergines into a sieve set over a bowl, and sprinkle a couple of teaspoons of salt over them. Leave for 10 minutes then thoroughly rinse off the salt under cold water. This will prevent the aubergines absorbing too much oil.

Cut the top and bottom off the fennel and remove the outer layer. As the layers are removed, you will be left with V-shaped pieces of fennel, which will need to be cut in half so that 2 slightly curved pieces remain. Trim these up so that they are as near to rectangular as possible and, if necessary, slice off some of the flesh if too thick. Cut into pieces the same size as the other vegetables.

Serves 4

3 medium aubergines

3 medium/large courgettes, as green as possible

salt and freshly ground black pepper

1 bulb of fennel

2 red peppers

10 black olives

extra virgin olive oil

3 teaspoons fresh thyme leaves

approximately 250g tomato fondue (see page 75)

10 fresh basil leaves

10 coriander seeds

oil from the tomato fondue

Preheat the grill. Top and tail the red peppers and remove the pith, seeds and any green (see page 122). Rub them with olive oil and arrange them, skin-side up, on the grill tray. Put them under the grill and leave them until they go black all over; don't worry, they will not be burnt but will have developed a lovely charred flavour. When blackened, put them into a bowl and cover tightly with clingfilm; leave for 5 minutes. You will then be able to peel them easily under cold running water. Once peeled, dice the flesh. Stone and finely chop the olives.

Have ready a fine-meshed sieve set over a bowl.

Heat a frying pan large enough to hold the diced aubergine in one layer. Add enough olive oil to cover the bottom of the pan by 1–2mm. When the oil is very hot, but not smoking, add the aubergines, cook for 4 minutes, then tip the contents of the pan into the sieve, allowing it to drain. Season with salt and pepper and add ½ teaspoon of thyme leaves. When drained, tip the aubergines into a bowl reserving their oil.

Using fresh olive oil, repeat the process with the courgettes, on a slightly lower heat, cooking for just 2 minutes as they will continue to cook after being removed from the pan. Drain, keeping the oil, season and add ½ teaspoon of thyme leaves.

Finally, cook the fennel in fresh oil, this time on a low to medium heat, for 6–8 minutes. Don't undercook the fennel, or its crunchiness will dominate the dish. Drain as before, keeping the oil.

To finish the dish, mix together all of the vegetables with the tomato fondue and the chopped olives. Finely slice the basil and add it to the other ingredients along with the rest of the thyme leaves and the coriander seeds.

Finally mix in the tomato fondue oil and the reserved oil from the fried vegetables to taste, season and serve.

If the ratatouille is to be eaten hot, reheat it in a moderate oven for 5 minutes.

★ Tip
This dish does not suit being made too long in advance: one day ahead maximum. If you do want to make it earlier, do not add the tomatoes or the acid contained in them will discolour the other vegetables and the ratatouille will lose its sweetness. Add them later.

Vegetables en Cocotte

'En cocotte' is a French cooking term. It is covered in the Sunday lunch section (page 153), as it primarily applies to meat, but it is also a fantastic way of cooking vegetables. With a little knowledge of how long it takes to cook each vegetable, this method of cooking will provide a fantastic dish with an integral, ready-made sauce. Following a few steps will make life easier. The recipe that follows is just an example of what can be done using these guidelines.

1. Make sure that the pot used is neither so big that the vegetables will get lost in it, particularly if adding any liquid, nor so small as to overcrowd the pan; the vegetables will not cook evenly.

2. Vegetables such as onions, potatoes and garlic will take longer to cook and will therefore need to go into the pan first.

3. Vegetables such as green peas, lettuces and broad beans take a lot less time to cook, and it may well be better to blanch these vegetables beforehand until you are confident about how long they all take. Add them towards the end, as they will already be cooked.

4. The same applies to fresh herbs. Rosemary, bay leaf and thyme can be added at the beginning, but the more delicate herbs such as parsley, chervil and coriander should be added towards the end.

5. If adding potatoes and they are to become crisp, precook them in unsalted boiling water until the point of a sharp knife penetrates them easily. Remember that these potatoes will not stay crisp if you add any liquid to the pan.

Set the oven to 180°C/gas mark 4.

Put some carrots into a casserole with a generous amount of butter and a few cloves of garlic. Add some fresh thyme or rosemary. Put the casserole into the oven.

After about half an hour, add some peeled and quartered turnips and some baby onions that have been blanched and peeled.

After another 20 minutes, add some green beans that have been blanched for 3 minutes and some tomatoes, peeled, deseeded and chopped.

Leave to cook for another 10 minutes, season them with salt and freshly ground black pepper and sprinkle over some chopped fresh herbs.

This will give you some idea of the method, but the possibilities are endless. Even a little bit of smoked bacon could be added.

Hopefully, having understood the contents of this chapter, a whole new world of possibilities will open up to you and your children. Wouldn't it be fantastic to think that you could walk around the local supermarket, greengrocer or farm shop and, with the children, choose a selection of the best vegetables that are available?

Fish

Now here is a food that is definitely one of the more problematic when it comes to our offspring. My son, Jack, would definitely not put fish as his food Top of the Pops. Our eldest daughter, Jessica, however, loves fish, especially clams, mussels and tuna. The strange thing about that is that my wife, who normally loves seafood, could not bear the thought of anything remotely fishy while she was pregnant with Jessica!

Fish is invariably introduced to children wrapped in something, be it breadcrumbs, batter or potato. There are probably two reasons for this. The first is that it is probably one of the surest ways to get children to actually eat fish. The second reason is a lot more sinister.

We live on an island, but are so void of fishmongers it is shocking. Most fish caught off British shores ends up in markets in France and Spain. On my first visit to the gigantic Paris market of Rungis, I was amazed to see that the best salmon in the market, and priced as such, came from Scotland. It is not Scottish salmon being one of the very best available that I would question, but the fact that one rarely finds salmon of this quality in England.

The demise of the local fishmonger can probably be attributed to two main factors: lack of demand, probably due to the cost of much fresh fish, and the general feeling that cooking fish involves a lot more preparation and knowledge than many other foods.

The term fresh fish is now becoming an ever-increasing misnomer. Most frozen fish is actually in a 'fresher' state than the majority of fresh fish to be found in the supermarkets. The reason for this is that the trawlers obviously need to net enough fish while out at sea to make it worth the trip, and this means that they will spend at least one week at sea. Fish destined for sale in our supermarkets as 'frozen' will be frozen on the boat, which means that the time between it being caught and being frozen will be relatively short. If fish is frozen while still in a state of rigor mortis, its freshness will be preserved and it will be in better condition than fish a few days old. The fish to be sold as 'fresh', however, will be refrigerated until the boat returns. By the time the trawlers have landed and the catch arrives on the refrigerated supermarket shelves, it could well be over a week old. Do you ever wonder why so-called fresh fish bought from these supermarkets never seems to last for longer than a couple of days?

For me, one of the beauties of really fresh fish is that it requires a lot less fiddling around with than one might think. Especially when, if you are lucky enough to have a local fishmonger, he will happily prepare the fish for you. The premise that fish involves a lot more preparation and knowledge than many other foods could not be further from the truth.

Simplicity is the key when you have good-quality fresh fish. Simply garnish it with one of many suitable recipes in this book, particularly in the vegetable and snack sections: the red pepper and anchovy recipe (page 53), confit tomatoes (page 57) or onion compote (page 55), for example, are delicious with all sorts of fish. What about some baked beans with cod and pea purée or even chips (pages 73, 233, 225)? Braised lentils (page 238), crushed potatoes (page 220) or ratatouille (page 244) would be a fantastic garnish with some salmon, red mullet or one of the risotto recipes on pages 92–107 – fish really is versatile.

Because of this versatility, this chapter has not been structured around recipes in the way the other chapters have. Instead it includes a range of cooking techniques for fish, suggesting the type of fish that would be best suited to that technique and listing some of the recipes that would make ideal accompaniments. This way you and your children will be free to try many different varieties of fish, cooked in different ways, perhaps finding success with something that the children thought they would not like.

★ Children's tip
It is important to get children to touch and smell the fish wherever possible. Even if they don't always eat it, our kids love to do this. Learning how to recognize a fresh fish gets your children involved from the beginning and will perhaps make them more ready to try something for the first time. We must not let any of our eating hang-ups pass on to our children. After all, how can we get them to try something new if we aren't prepared to be open-minded ourselves?

The following points are important when judging the freshness of a fish:

- The eyes should be clear, bright and shiny, not at all dull and sunken.
- Lift up the gills: they should be red and clean, not grey.

- Smell the fish: fresh fish has almost no smell whatsoever, except perhaps a faint smell of the sea; if it is in any way strong-smelling, reject it.
- Check for any abrasions, cuts or scars, which may mean that the fish has been thrown around too much either in the process of being caught or in the handling afterwards.
- The flesh should be tight and 'spring' back when you press it, not at all flaccid.

Cooking times

Many cookery books will give approximate cooking times per weight of fish. The problem is that, as with meat, going by cooking times alone will invariably produce unsuccessful results. As Alan Davidson points out in *The Oxford Companion to Food*: 'The time taken for heat to penetrate an object is not in simple proportion to its thickness but to the square of its thickness.' This means that a piece of fish or meat that is twice as thick as another will actually take four times as long to cook. Once again a probe (see page 26) will make life very easy, and fish cookery foolproof. This will, of course, become even easier with experience.

This may all sound like a bit of a chore. Believe me, it will be far less so than following a recipe, carefully calculating the cooking time and ending up with either still raw or very over-cooked fish.

If, for any reason, a probe is not available, it would still be preferable to rely on your own judgement rather than following time-per-kilo charts.

Cooking techniques

With all these techniques, the most important thing to remember is not to overcook the fish – a problem far too often encountered, even in many good restaurants. Salmon, for example, cooked so that it is still opaque in the middle, is, contrary to what many people believe, not raw and is not unhealthy. It is wonderfully moist and has a fantastic texture.

It is also very important to remember that because fish has no connective tissue as such and because of the way the flesh is structured, it will carry on cooking after it is removed from the heat source. It is better, therefore, to stop cooking it a minute or two before it is ready and leave it to rest before serving. Grilled or roasted red mullet fillets from a medium-sized fish will, for example, change in no time from appearing raw in the centre to being overcooked after being removed from the heat.

An easy way of telling whether a piece of fish is overcooked is when white, milky dots form on its surface (this is, in effect, albumen coagulating). Unfortunately, by this time it is already overcooked!

Poaching

This technique basically involves cooking the fish in hot liquid. It is a very delicate method of cooking and has the benefit that the pan can be brought to the table for serving.

The important thing is to ensure that the poaching liquid

does not get too hot; it definitely must not boil, or the fish will become overcooked and dried out, losing all its wonderfully delicate texture. When poaching a whole fish it is advisable to put it in the cold liquid and bring it up to the required temperature, as this will allow a longer time for the fish to take on some of the flavour of the poaching liquid. Whether the fish is to be eaten hot or cold, you are better off leaving it in the liquid until you are about to serve it or, in the case of fish that is to be served cold, at least until it cools down.

As the internal temperature of the fish passes 42°C, the proteins begin to contract, squeezing out moisture and eventually causing the fish to become overcooked and dry. Ideally, maintaining the temperature of the cooking water a few degrees above the desired internal temperature of the fish would be perfect. A probe will be very useful here. Otherwise don't worry, just keep the liquid hot but not simmering.

This method suits whole fish or bigger pieces of fish on the bone. I know that many people are a little uncomfortable with eating fish on the bone – however, please give it a try. The fish will taste better and be more tender, as the bone will protect the flesh from drying out.

The poaching liquid can be varied to taste. Some examples are:

- The classical court-bouillon, which is, in effect, water flavoured with vegetables, herbs and sometimes spices such as star anise, lightly acidulated with white wine and lemon juice.
- A similar liquid but made with an increased quantity of red wine.

- Stock, the classic one being fish stock, although meat stock, chicken stock or the liquid from a light stew can work quite well.
- Milk works well for poaching fish, as it tends to retain the colour in salmon, for example, and lends itself to being flavoured. Try star anise, cloves, pepper, cinnamon, nutmeg and some herbs; but do not add any salt or acid as it will curdle the milk.

Confit

Confit is, essentially, poaching in oil at a low temperature and is a technique that we use quite a lot at the restaurant. We do, however, have the benefit of equipment such as stirred water baths that maintain a temperature of 45°C. The fish cooks in this and can take quite a long time – half an hour for a 250g skinless salmon fillet, for example. It looks opaque when done, almost raw, but the flesh flakes easily and the texture is incomparable.

Please try this. Just make sure that the skinless salmon fillet is relatively even in shape and at least 2.5cm thick (the fishmonger will do this for you). Bring the olive oil to 45°C, put in the salmon fillets and cook for about 25 minutes. The fish will still look undercooked but will flake beautifully.

The poach-grill method for fish with skin on works very well when cooking with this technique: the fish – red mullet, for example – comes out of the oil when cooked and goes straight into a very hot non-stick pan, skin side down, for a few seconds to break the skin down.

The oil used can vary: olive oil, for example, works very well and can be flavoured with all sorts of things, ranging from jasmine tea to rosemary and vanilla. You could use goose fat, sesame oil or even butter, which, although delicious, is not, for obvious reasons, best for you or your children on a regular basis.

Steaming

For this technique use a steamer, or, failing that, a colander that will sit perfectly over the pan containing the liquid. It is important, however, to make sure that it does sit perfectly or the fish will not cook evenly.

Once again, there is a wide range of flavourings that can be put into the liquid: salt, herbs and lemon zest are the most obvious, although alcohol, in the form of wine, sherry or vermouth, and a few spices can also be added.

With steaming, it is very important to be aware that, as steam is hotter than water, the fish will cook very quickly, and the point when there is enough residual heat in the fish will happen relatively suddenly. It is therefore advisable to remove it from the steam a little while before it is cooked, allowing the residual heat to finish the cooking process. This method is only foolproof if using a probe. If you are using one (see page 26), remove the fish when it is at 38°C.

Baking, Pot-roasting and Roasting

This is the same principle as is used for meats (see the pot-roast pork recipe, page 153). It generally works better for bigger pieces, and particularly for whole fish, as it needs to spend long enough on the bed of aromatics for some interplay of flavours to happen. As with poaching, this method of cooking allows the whole pot to be brought to the table for serving, together with all its aromas!

The basic principle is quite simple. First season the fish with salt and freshly ground black pepper and, if you like, colour it in foaming butter in a casserole. Then remove the fish from the casserole and put in whatever vegetables, herbs and spices you wish. These vegetables can be pre- or part-cooked depending on how long they will take and their size. Whole baby potatoes, for example, will probably require some precooking, as will carrots; very thinly sliced potatoes, however, will be fine with a whole fish.

Put the fish back in, add a little wine or other liquid, put the lid on the casserole, and put it into the oven at 70°C/gas mark $^1/_8$ or lower. Do not cook at too high a temperature, or by the time that the aromatics have begun to play their part, the fish will have overcooked. The steam that builds up helps the fish retain moisture, and the sealed dish concentrates the aromas.

The pan can be left uncovered if you prefer: this will create a more gentle cooking environment but more of the flavour will be lost.

This method works well for slightly more dense-textured fish, such as turbot (although it is expensive and not always easy to get hold of) and monkfish.

If adding a little liquid to the pan, the dish can be finished with a knob of butter, providing a wonderful sauce.

Frying

Many restaurants will say on the menu that a particular fish has been roasted, or pan-roasted or, in the worst case, pan-fried! This tends to be restaurant-speak, as to roast something it needs to be put into or on a pan anyway and the fish, in nearly every case, will have been half roasted and half fried. By the nature of frying itself, a pan is required; it is like saying salmon fish or port wine!

Frying works very well with fillets of fish, particularly if they have their skin on, as the more delicate flesh will be protected from the direct heat of the pan.

The fat you choose is quite important for both flavour and heating capabilities. Groundnut oil can withstand relatively high temperatures while butter, although imparting a richer, nutty flavour, will burn at a much lower temperature. Clarified butter can work well, as it can sustain higher temperatures.

Frying has a second advantage: fantastically crispy skin. I cannot see why anyone does not like crisp fish skin, and my daughter adores it. A few years ago in France, a new method of cooking fish appeared; it was called 'à la unilatéral' and basically involved cooking a fillet of fish with its skin on in a non-stick pan on the skin side only, thus protecting the more delicate, flesh side of the fillet from drying out. Cooking fish in this manner gave another dimension to the end result. The fish itself has a heat variation from one side to the other and also a textural one; from cooked to almost raw.

★ **Tip**

Here is an interesting experiment. Take a liquid that is quite thick, for example, the pea purée on page 233. Split the purée into 3 parts. Leave one third cold and heat the other two up – one to tepid and the other quite hot. Now taste the three purées and they will all have slightly different characteristics.

Many restaurants now adopt this technique, although not quite in the way the original method was intended. The fish is finished off in the oven for a few minutes. The pan never comes into direct contact with the flesh.

This process is very quick, and a little care needs to be taken to get the right surface temperature – too cold and the skin will not crisp up, too hot and the fillet will curl up and the skin will burn. The pan does, however, need to be hot.

Once again, the fish can be placed on a bed of something – very finely sliced fennel and chopped olives for example – before going into the oven, thus accentuating the variation in heat, texture and flavour.

Deep-frying

Here a piece of fish is first coated in a batter (to prevent the heat of the oil from overcooking it) then plunged into very hot oil or dripping as in some fish and chip shops. It is important, when deep-frying, that the batter completely coats the fish.

Grilling

Probably the quickest and most simple way of cooking fish. It also happens to be the easiest way to overcook it, particularly whole fish: by the time the middle has cooked, there is a good chance that the outside will be overcooked.

Grilling can work pretty well on the barbecue when you can cook over vines or herbs. You will also be able to achieve a less aggressive heat. When cooking fish on a barbecue, leave the skin on the fish for protection and also, wherever possible, leave the scales on. Just make sure that they are removed before eating!

When grilling a whole fish, make a few cuts across the flesh on each side of the fish to facilitate a more even cooking. The thickness of fish will vary considerably along its length, and when considering that a piece of fish twice as thick as another will take four times as long to cook (see page 256) it is easy to see that there will be a huge difference in cooking time for various areas of the same fish.

It is here that the low-temperature technique again wins over, because the outer parts of the fish do not have to be subjected to excessive temperatures for too long a period in order to achieve the required temperature at the centre of the thickest parts of the flesh.

Marinating

Many countries around the world have their own versions of marinating or curing fish. Escabeche, which can be used for meat as well, has been popular in Spain for centuries. It basically involves cooking (usually frying) a piece of fish or meat, often lightly floured, and then placing it in a warm or room-temperature marinade, often involving sherry vinegar and olive oil.

Ceviche, from South America, takes raw fish and marinates it with olive oil and lemon or lime juice. This in effect 'cooks' the fish. If the fish is left in the marinade for too long, however, it will be overcooked. Although the fish itself is not subjected to any heat, the action of the lemon or lime juice has the same effect on the proteins in the flesh as does the application of heat.

'Minute'

This is a method where very thinly sliced fish is placed on a serving plate and put into a hot oven (180°C/gas mark 4) for 1–2 minutes. This hot dinner plate method is sometimes used to finish the cooking of a fillet of fish. For example, a fillet of red mullet that has been cooked, skin-side down only, in a frying pan, with the flesh side still a little underdone, is placed flesh side down on a hot dinner plate. The heat of the plate, while it is being taken to the table, will finish off the cooking of the fish.

Baked in Salt

With this method a whole fish is placed in a baking tray lined with moist, coarse sea salt. The fish itself is then covered in salt, tightly packed, and baked. When done, the salt forms a solid crust that needs to be cracked open, releasing the wonderful aromas of the fish.

Herbs can be added, but this method suits ultra-fresh fish of the more grand varieties – turbot, for example – and in this case it is best to let the fish speak for itself.

Roasted in a Salt Crust

This is essentially the same method as for chicken in a salt crust (page 162). Again, this works well with bigger pieces of fish, as by the time a crust has formed smaller fish will be over-cooked. Fish cooked in salt has its skin left on and removed when serving, as this part will be salty.

Recipes

★ **Children's tip**

In terms of recipes for fish, it is probably best to test the water first (excuse the pun!). You may well be lucky enough to have children who adore fish. If, however, you are like me and have a mixed bag, or simply non-believers, then some experimenting will need to be done.

As with all ingredients, the more your children can touch and learn about the raw ingredient, the more chance there is of getting them to eat it. Things will definitely be made easier in this regard if a local fishmonger is to hand. Take the children with you when buying the fish. If the fishmonger will be filleting the fish for you, let your children look, smell and touch the fish first – he will be only too pleased that they are interested.

Ask the fishmonger to show them how to recognize fresh fish. They will be more likely to listen to him (no offence!).

Look no further than the recipes in this book to give you a wide range of dishes to accompany the fish.

To start with, rather than looking particularly at the balance of the dish itself, it may be an idea to do the following. Take one of the dishes from the vegetable or grain section (without meat) that are particular favourites and serve it with the fish your child is most likely to eat. For example, my daughter likes fish but particularly loves prawns, clams and tuna fish. Any of these with the gratin dauphinois on page 222 would be a real treat. Mackerel, however, though she will eat it, does not reach the premier league in her taste table.

My son, on the other hand, will in some cases eat freshly

cooked tuna fish but cannot stand the tinned variety. (Although because it contains bacon, he will eat tuna with the carbonara recipe on page 84).

Bearing these points in mind, there is quite a bit of scope for experimenting: a little flaked, lightly cooked fish such as cod, salmon or tuna could be added to one of the soup recipes – tomato (page 119), leek and potato (page 127) or butternut (page 130).

Here are some suggestions to get started, including the methods of cooking that you could choose.

Sauté of Squid with Ratatouille

Cut up some squid and marinate in a little olive oil with lemon juice, garlic and thyme for a couple of hours. Then sauté briefly in very hot oil (a couple of minutes is ample).

This can be served on or mixed with ratatouille (page 244). If mixed, the dish is good served cold or at room temperature.

The sautéd squid, with or without the ratatouille, would be equally delicious stirred into the basic risotto (page 98), some couscous (page 109) or even pasta (page 89). If mixing with pasta, do it while the pasta is still hot so that there is a better exchange of flavours.

Fillet of Salmon with Crushed Potatoes

A like or dislike for crispy salmon skin will determine the cooking method here. For example, a skinless salmon fillet will not have protection from an aggressive heat source and will not suit being cooked unilaterally.

With a slightly thicker piece of fish, cook it skin-side down and just before serving turn the fish over for a few seconds.

If you have a skinless piece of salmon, cook it using the confit method (see page 259).

Adding generous amounts of fresh rosemary to the oil will give a wonderfully rustic note to the fish.

Serve it with crushed potatoes (page 220) and a little olive oil.

Red Mullet, Tart Pissaladière

This is a very easy dish to make if some of the necessary staples are to hand in the fridge. If not, it will take a bit of work from the 'team'.

Some onion compote (page 55), confit tomatoes (page 57) and confit garlic (page 196) are needed for this recipe. In addition to this, you will need to buy a small packet of puff pastry, some marinated (not salted) anchovies and some black olives.

On a floured work surface, roll out the puff pastry to a thickness of a couple of millimetres. Put it on a baking tray, prick it with a fork and leave to rest in the fridge for a couple of hours.

Preheat the oven to 190°C/gas mark 5. Take the pastry out of the fridge. Using a 12cm pastry cutter or, failing that, an up-turned saucer and a sharp knife, cut 4 discs of pastry. Lay a sheet of parchment paper on a baking tray and place the pastry discs on top. Cover the discs with more parchment paper and place another tray on top to prevent the bases from rising. Cook for about 20 minutes, turning the discs over half-way through, then remove from the oven and allow to cool a little. Reduce the oven to 150°/gas mark 2.

Spread the bottom of each base with some onion compote and top with a slice or two of confit tomato. Lay a couple of anchovies over the tomatoes along with some olive halves. Finally, top with a fillet of red mullet. Put back into the oven and cook for approximately 5–8 minutes.

Remember to remove the fish from the oven while still a little underdone, as it will continue to cook after you take it out.

A spoonful of marinated peppers (page 53) would make a delicious accompaniment.

★ Variation

If feeling adventurous, make one big tart and cook a couple of whole fish on top.

Mullet livers are delicious, and although this may not be the most tasty-sounding food, please try them: they are fantastic.

Red mullet is also a great accompaniment to red wine risotto (page 106). This time the fish, if using fillets, could be cooked skin-side down or lightly grilled.

Pot-roast Cod

Place a large piece of cod on a bed of onions and garlic, cooked together until soft (even a little browned), and a generous amount of fresh thyme. Add a few precooked new potatoes. Cover and cook in a warm oven (about 120°C/gas mark 1/4) for about 15 minutes.

Remove the fish from the pan when it is cooked, and deglaze the pan with a little white wine and/or vermouth, adding a touch of water and a knob of butter to the pan to make the sauce. Place the fish back on top and bring the pot to the table.

Why not introduce some meat to the pot-roast cod? A scattering of smoked bacon lardons would be nice.

★ **Variation**

Fish and meat combinations can work really well together. If, by any chance, some braised oxtail (page 184) is available, reserve any sauce left over. It's fantastic with grilled or sautéd squid, or with red mullet or sea bass, and served with braised lettuce (page 207).

Desserts

This is definitely one area of cooking in which children will require little encouragement to get involved. The biggest problem will probably be persuading them to clean up afterwards!

Desserts are different from many other areas of cooking in that it is more difficult to stray from a recipe. In many cases, ingredients are there for reasons other than taste. Eggs, for example, play numerous roles, ranging from thickening to incorporating air and lightness in a dessert. Even sugar often contributes more than sweetness; in custard, for example, it interferes with the egg proteins, helping to prevent them coagulating.

Desserts need little by way of an introduction, except perhaps to say that it is the area in which many cookery books aimed at or involving children seem to fall into the same trap. Most of the recipes will be based on baking and will follow the theory that all kids love kneading dough and playing with a rolling pin. You should credit children with more intelligence than that and give them a range of recipes that also require other jobs.

★ Children's tip

Show the children the importance of measuring, both solids and liquids, using scales and measuring jugs; make sure that both are on a level surface before using them! The importance of having an accurate set of scales and an oven thermometer cannot be emphasized enough. My wife was testing the recipe for the chocolate fondant and the rice pudding. The fondant failed due to the oven being 25° out from the dial, and the rice pudding was far too runny because our scales were not accurate with smaller measures.

The best way to test scales is by simply weighing something whose weight is already known. If the scales are not accurate, then, wherever possible, use the information on the packaging of the ingredients that you will be using. For example, packets of butter are normally calibrated and chocolate bars come in squares: simply divide the weight of the bar by the number of squares for the weight of each one. This could even become part of your child's maths lesson!

I think you definitely need to follow the seasons with desserts: no strawberries at Christmas. Fruits that don't grow in this country are the exceptions to this rule, for example, pineapples, bananas and mangoes, but try to make sure that they are being eaten within what would be their own season in their country of origin. This in itself is a good exercise, as it will give children more awareness of other countries' seasons as well as our own (it will probably educate many of us parents as well!).

Involve the children in the buying of fruits, and teach them what to look for in terms of quality and freshness, so that they will be able, with touch and smell, to determine the quality and as importantly, the ripeness of that fruit.

At the restaurant we use unrefined sugar for nearly all our desserts. Available from most supermarkets, it is infinitely better than refined sugar, with a wonderfully old-fashioned aroma of molasses.

As adults, we are drawn back to childhood tastes. For example, when I was a child, growing up in London, there was an ice-cream parlour on the Edgware Road called the Regent Snack Bar. It was run by a couple of big Italians in white coats and won awards for its ice-creams. Every Saturday morning, my grandmother would take my sister and me to Church Street market off the Edgware Road. This would have been a major drag if it hadn't been for the fact that we were treated to a tub of vanilla ice-cream from the Regent Snack Bar on the way home. Each little plastic tub was put into a brown paper bag along with a miniature wooden spoon; I couldn't wait to get home! I never forgot the taste of this ice-cream and spent a long time trying to find out what it was that was so special about it. Eventually I decided that it had to be the addition of a few coffee beans when making the custard base that did it!

This is the influence for the vanilla ice-cream recipe in this chapter. Some recipe books will tell you that you can make ice-cream by hand, stirring the mixture every half an hour or so until it hardens, but the result, especially for this recipe, will just not be the same. It is a lot of work for a compromise. If, however, you do have an ice-cream machine please give it a go; it will certainly be better than any equivalent on the shelves.

Vanilla Ice-cream

There is no cream in this recipe and it has a low sugar content. At the restaurant we try to make all our ice-creams this way, as you get a more dense texture, heightening the flavour. The ice-cream is not at all chewy through excess sweetness and does not leave a fatty coating in the mouth.

Because of the reduced sugar and fat content, the quantity of egg yolk has been increased and skimmed milk powder has been added. This stops the ice-cream from crystallizing and becoming icy or grainy. The result is a wonderfully rich ice-cream that is at the same time very light and clean and melts almost instantly in the mouth.

Do not balk at the number of vanilla pods: they are expensive, but they can be cut down if absolutely necessary.

Make the custard base the day before churning it, as the flavour and texture are improved by one day of 'resting'. In the absence of an ice-cream machine, all is not lost. You will have delicious custard to hand instead of using something out of a packet.

★ **Tip**

A few words on egg sizes. Although not absolutely crucial in most of these recipes, the amount of whole eggs, yolks or whites in a recipe can be vital. All the eggs used in the following recipes are medium-sized, with the yolk weighing 20g and the white 30g.

The recipe for the fondant gives the exact weight for the amount of egg white required. This system makes it a little easier to know what to do with leftover egg whites, for example. Egg whites freeze pretty well, and knowing the weight of each white means that you will not be looking at your tub of whites wondering how much 8 egg whites, for example, would look like!

Makes approximately 2 litres

6 vanilla pods (this quantity can be reduced if you wish)

625ml whole milk

50g skimmed milk powder

120g unrefined caster sugar

10 whole coffee beans

6 medium egg yolks

Place the vanilla pods on a chopping board and run a small, sharp knife along the length of each pod, cutting it in half. Use the knife to scrape out the seeds. Put the seeds into the whisking bowl of an electric mixer and add the empty pods to the milk. In the absence of an electric mixer, a good-sized mixing-bowl with a rounded base will do.

Pour the milk and vanilla pods into a casserole of at least 1.5 litre capacity. Add the milk powder, a dessertspoon of the sugar and the coffee beans. Place the casserole on a medium heat and bring the milk to the boil. As soon as it boils, turn the heat down and allow the milk to simmer for 5 minutes. Remove from the heat and leave to infuse for 20 minutes.

Meanwhile, add the egg yolks to the vanilla seeds in the whisking bowl, along with the remaining sugar. Turn the machine to full speed and beat until the mixture whitens. This will take at least 10 minutes – a bit unfortunate for your arms if you are doing it by hand! When the mixture has turned white and significantly increased in volume, place the casserole back on a medium heat and return the liquid to a simmer. Turn the heat down to low, then immediately pour this liquid very gently, pods and all, on to the egg mixture while still beating.

Return this mixture to the casserole and place on a low heat. Stir continuously, preferably with a flat-bottomed wooden spoon. It is essential that the mixture does not boil, or it will become grainy. The custard is ready when it passes the spoon test: dip a wooden spoon into the mixture and lift it out. Holding the spoon horizontally, draw a line along the back of the spoon with your finger and if it retains its shape, the custard is ready.

Have ready a bowl large enough to fit the mixture in and sit it in a larger bowl containing ice and a little cold water. When the custard is ready, pour it into the bowl and continue stirring for a few minutes until it is cold. Strain through a fine-meshed sieve. At this point the custard can be stored in a sealed container in the fridge for up to 2 days maximum. Make sure that it is thoroughly mixed so that the vanilla seeds that have fallen to the bottom are evenly distributed.

Churn the custard in your ice-cream machine and place in the freezer, with some clingfilm pressed on to the surface of the ice-cream. Leave in the freezer for 2 hours before serving.

Tarte Tatin

The story behind this is that the Tatin sisters, who ran a simple restaurant in the Loire valley of France, were making an apple tart and forgot to line the tin first. Instead of starting the recipe again, they decided to put the pastry on top and continue cooking it, tipping it upside-down at the end.

If this story is true, it must be one of the best gastronomic mistakes ever made, for it has given us a wonderful dessert.

Making puff pastry can be rewarding, but it does need time and patience. With bought puff pastry, which works perfectly well for this dish, the recipe could not be simpler. It has only 3 ingredients other than the pastry: apples, sugar and butter. By following a few basic principles, this is one of those dishes where the end result belies its simplicity.

A straight-sided, heavy-bottomed pan is needed for this so that the edges of the pastry can be tucked under the apples. The thick base is important, as it will be a more efficient conductor of heat and less likely than a thin pan to have a hot spot where the caramel may burn. Do not be too concerned about the exact size of the pan, as to a certain extent the quantity of the ingredients can be adjusted, making a larger or smaller Tatin.

Use an apple such as a Cox or Braeburn rather than a Granny Smith.

The quantities given are sufficient for a 20cm pan, and will comfortably feed 4

80g unsalted butter

100g unrefined caster sugar

5–6 Cox or Braeburn apples (the wedges of apple need to be packed tightly into the pan so the quantity of apples required will depend on the size of the apples themselves)

flour for rolling out the pastry

1 packet of frozen puff pastry, made with butter if possible

Leave the butter to soften slightly then spread it evenly over the bottom of the pan. Sprinkle the sugar over the butter.

Peel the apples, cut in half through the stem and remove the core. Cut each half into 3 wedges. Now pack the apples in the pan side by side, pointing upwards. There should be no gaps anywhere in the pan. Put the pan on a medium heat.

The sugar and butter in the pan will begin to bubble and will gradually turn to a light golden colour. Using the underside of a slightly smaller pan, press down evenly on the apples. Be careful that the sugar/butter mix does not get forced over the sides of the pan on to your cooker! When it begins to darken a little more, remove the pan from the heat and set aside. Preheat the oven to 180°C/gas mark 4. On a lightly floured work surface, roll out the pastry to a thickness of 2–3mm. Cut the rolled pastry to a disc 1cm larger than the diameter of the pan.

When the apples have cooled down enough to handle, roll the pastry around your rolling pin, hold it over the pan and unroll it so that it drops on to the apples. Carefully tuck the pastry under the apples and make several holes in it with a small sharp knife.

Put the pan in the preheated oven for about 35 minutes. When ready, the pastry should turn a light golden brown colour. Remove the pan from the oven to cool down, but make sure that you turn the Tatin out while it is still warm, otherwise it will stick to the pan. To turn out the Tatin, cover the top of the pan with an upturned plate large enough to hold the tart. Quickly, but carefully, tip the pan upside down and shake gently if necessary. Tell your children to listen out for the really welcoming flopping sound as the tart slips out and on to the plate.

★ Children's tip
Be careful when turning out the tart, especially if it is one of your little helpers who will be doing it as the caramel will keep its heat and may burn.

Serve the Tatin with cream, ice-cream or custard. A few lightly roasted hazelnuts added to the pan before topping with the pastry work quite nicely.

★ Variation
Nowadays there are many variations of this dish, using, among other things, pears, apricots, bananas and mangoes. Savoury Tatins can be made using, for example, shallots, chicory or courgettes. The nectarine recipe that follows can be adapted to peaches or apricots and turned into a tarte Tatin, as we do at the Fat Duck.

Nectarines Poached with Star Anise and Rosemary

The sugar content of the syrup can be reduced when poaching fruits, but below a certain level the fruit will become mushy as the cell walls collapse. The syrup creates a form of barrier, which is why tinned fruit is always more dense in texture.

The herbs and spices in this poaching syrup give a wonderful character to the fruit. Vary them as you wish.

For this recipe you will need to make a cartouche (see page 50).

First, make the syrup; simply put the water and sugar in a casserole large enough to hold the nectarines in one layer. On a high heat, bring to the boil, stirring, and remove from the heat when the sugar has dissolved.

Cut the vanilla pod in half, scrape out the seeds and put the pod, along with the seeds, into the casserole. Add the rest of the ingredients to the pan and cover with a cartouche so that some syrup sits on top of it, keeping the fruits submerged. Bring the liquid to a gentle simmer, then remove from the heat. Leave the fruit to cool down in this liquid.

Store the nectarines in the liquid until needed. They will keep well in the fridge for a week.

The short cooking time given for the nectarines is so that

Serves 4–6 depending on the size of the nectarines

1 vanilla pod

8 ripe nectarines

5 whole star anise, broken up

8 sprigs of fresh rosemary

10 fresh bay leaves

zest of 1 lemon

For the syrup

2 litres water

750g unrefined caster sugar

they can then be used for a tarte Tatin, where they will be cooked a second time in the oven. If they are not going to be used in a Tatin, it is advisable to cook them on a bare simmer for 10 minutes before leaving them to cool down.

Tarte Tatin of Nectarines with Star Anise and Rosemary

Prepare the fruit as on page 286, then cut in half and remove the stones.

Follow the recipe for tarte Tatin see page (283–4).

As a variation, add a few almonds along with the nectarines before topping with the pastry.

Caramelized Puff Pastries

This is a great, simple way of making sweet biscuits using bought frozen puff pastry. It's ideal for kids to make.

Simply roll out a little puff pastry as thin as possible, but instead of using flour to prevent sticking, use icing sugar.

Next, roll the sheet of pastry up to form a cylinder 3–4cm in diameter and cut it into thin discs. Roll these discs as thin as possible, again using icing sugar.

Put them into the fridge for an hour or into the freezer for half an hour; this will stop them shrinking too much when they are cooking.

Preheat the oven to 220°C/gas mark 7 and place the cold pastry on parchment paper, on a baking sheet. Bake until golden.

While the biscuits are cooking, place a flat-bottomed pan, with a base large enough to cover a biscuit, in the freezer for about 10 seconds. When the biscuits are ready, remove the baking sheet from the oven and, using the cold pan, press hard on each biscuit. This will keep the biscuits as thin as possible.

These are delicious sprinkled with a little ground cinnamon.

Pain Perdu

This is a sweet French version of eggy-bread. It is a real children's favourite – watch in joy as they transfer the soaked bread from the bowl to the frying pan, dripping the sticky egg and milk mix across the floor and the work surface. You love them really!

If you can get hold of it, brioche is delicious for this. Serve the pain perdu with some fruit, poached, roasted or fried (see next recipe), a little milk jam (page 319), or just eat it on its own.

The only problem with this recipe is that your children will begin by pestering you to make it all the time, then, after a few goes, will be doing it themselves . . . just before their dinner!

Serves 4

4 slices of bread (ideally, leave the slices to dry for an hour or so)
130g unsalted butter
3 eggs
250ml whole milk
100g unrefined caster sugar

Put the butter into a pan and place on a medium heat. Let it completely melt and bubble up. Remove it from the heat and allow it to sit for 5 minutes, then carefully skim off the white foam on the surface and pour through a fine sieve (a tea-strainer will do), leaving behind the small particles of solids that have sunk to the bottom. This essentially removes the milky caseins and other particles that form the little burnt bits when the butter gets too hot. This is called clarified butter and can be heated to a higher temperature than normal butter.

In a bowl, mix together the eggs, milk, and 20g of the sugar. Trim the 4 slices of bread of their crusts and dip in this mix.

Heat the butter on a medium heat and add the bread. Cook quickly on both sides and, when golden, sprinkle over the remaining sugar. As soon as the slices have caramelized, they will be ready.

Pears in Butter

Pears have a wonderful affinity with star anise. This recipe is so simple and would be great with some pain perdu (see previous recipe).

This time the butter is not clarified, as the required temperature is not as high as is needed to cook the pain perdu. Also, a little bit of the flavour derived from the caseins colouring is a wanted addition to the dish.

These will need to be cooked at the last minute, but as they are really easy to do this is no great problem. Just bear in mind that the cooking time will vary depending on the type and ripeness of the fruit.

Allow 1 pear per person. To prepare them, simply cut each one in half lengthways and then each half into 3 equal segments; trim out the core but leave the skin on.

Put a generous amount of unsalted butter in a frying pan along with a couple of star anise, broken up. When the butter begins to foam and just starts to colour, add the pear slices and cook on a medium heat. Keep the butter golden and foaming but do not let it get too hot.

After about 5 minutes, check the pears – if they have lightly browned, turn them over. Serve as soon as they are ready.

Strawberry Soup

This recipe is part of a dish that is on the menu at the Fat Duck in season. Do give it a try, but please do it in the strawberry season. As well as quality, there is something quite magical about eating this during the English summer. Make sure that you buy the fruit no more than a day in advance, as they deteriorate really quickly.

★ **Children's tip**
Show the children how to spot a good strawberry – bright red in colour with a vivid green stem. Check that there are no blemishes or bruises on the strawberries. Contrary to popular belief, large, uniform strawberries are not a sign of quality. More often than not they are a result of laboratory-controlled agriculture.

If orange-flower water is not available, use rose water, which most chemists sell. Both of these ingredients are optional. You might want to omit the flower water the first time that you make this, as it could be too perfumed for your kids. Although, having said that, orange-flower water is still used to make a soothing sugared child's drink in many parts of Europe. In Spain, it is also put on children's pillows to give a comforting night-time aroma.

This recipe may seem rather lengthy, but the results will not disappoint. The concentration of flavour is amazing.

The strawberry juice can be omitted, although it is great as a base for making drinks or for pouring over ice-cream. It can even be added to the rice pudding recipe on page 305. It does keep very well.

★ **Tip**

Even if you are a bit short of time and cannot do this recipe, you will be surprised at how much the flavour of the strawberries can be heightened just by sprinkling some unrefined caster sugar over them half an hour before serving. If you have not read it already, have a quick read of the findings of a recent experiment regarding straw-berries on page 71.

Remember, when preparing strawberries, to hull them just before you macerate or use them. Do not wash them before hulling, or they will absorb water, destroying their taste and texture.

Try this recipe replacing the strawberries with rhubarb – it works brilliantly.

If doing the whole recipe, including the juice, begin the day before. Some muslin will also be needed.

Wash, hull and quarter the strawberries, put them into a metal bowl and sprinkle them with the icing sugar. Set this bowl over a saucepan of very gently simmering water, cover with cling-film, and leave for 1½ hours. Pour the contents of the bowl on to a large piece of muslin set over a bowl. Tie up the corners of the muslin and hang up over the bowl to catch all of the juice.

For the strawberry juice
500g strawberries
1 tablespoon icing sugar
1 tablespoon water

Hull and quarter the strawberries and put them into a bowl. Add the sugar and pour over the strawberry juice; leave this mix to macerate for 2 hours.

Zest the orange and lemon, taking care to discard all of the white pith which would make the liquid bitter. Juice the fruits and reserve.

Meanwhile, bring the red wine to the boil and immediately flame it with a match or, better still, a blowtorch. When the flames have ceased, add the zest and juice of the orange and lemon and boil to reduce the mixture by half. Strain this liquid and set aside to cool.

In a liquidizer, combine the macerated strawberries with the red wine reduction and blend.

Finishing the dish is the fun part, as it involves the taste-buds. Add the orange-flower water, about 1 tablespoon to begin with. A little more sugar may be needed along with some orange juice, depending on the ripeness and quality of the strawberries. The important thing here is to keep on tasting to get the right balance. Give the soup a really good blend and finish off by adding the black pepper to taste.

Now there are the following options:

1. Hang the soup in muslin again overnight. This will produce a wonderfully concentrated essence of strawberry.
2. Pass the soup through a fine-mesh sieve.
3. Serve it as it is, adding extra strawberries for texture if required.

For the soup
500g strawberries
1 tablespoon unrefined caster sugar
strawberry juice (see above)
1 orange
1 lemon
125ml fruity red wine
orange-flower water to taste
freshly ground black pepper
extra virgin olive oil

To serve, dribble over a little best-quality virgin olive oil. Finally, if feeling adventurous, finish the dish by sprinkling over some freshly picked rose petals!

Chocolate Fondant

This is one of those recipes that never fail to impress. Especially when made by your children.

I have used egg whites instead of yolks, as the yolk has a mouth-coating quality that tends to mask the purity of the chocolate (think of the feeling in the mouth eating a fried or boiled egg yolk). It is partly because of this that sugar is unnecessary in this recipe.

When making chocolate desserts, buy the best-quality bitter chocolate that you can get hold of – such as Valrhona. Waitrose bitter chocolate is one of the best supermarket ones.

If possible, get hold of some silicon paper, which will make life easier; otherwise, greaseproof paper will do the trick.

If these fondants are to be turned out, metal ring moulds without a base will be needed. When they are ready, just slide the rings off. If you haven't got anything like this, you can make them yourself: wash a small can, for example, a baked bean can, and simply cut off the top and bottom. Use one of the tin openers which cut the whole top off, so that it does not leave a protruding lip that will catch as it is lifted off the fondant.

If the fondants are not to be turned out, fill small ramekins with the mixture and serve in the ramekins.

★ **Variation**
This recipe is also delicious served uncooked as a mousse; it will need about 3 hours to set in the fridge. If doing this, incorporate 30ml of

cold water into the mix to prevent the flavour being too intense. Try a comparison to see which version your children prefer. Just make a batch of fondants and cook only half of them. Then taste them all together.

Fills 6 × 8cm diameter ramekins to a depth of approximately 5cm

240g best-quality bitter chocolate

100g unsalted butter

230g egg white (this equates to 7 medium-sized egg whites)

Preheat the oven to 200°C/gas mark 6.

With a knife, chop the chocolate into small pieces and cut the butter into small cubes – this will make it melt more evenly. Melt the butter and chocolate together, either in a microwave or in a bowl set over lightly simmering water. If using a microwave, be careful not to overheat as the butter will get too hot and may cause the mix to become grainy. If using a bowl over water, put the water into a pan whose diameter does not allow the bowl to come into contact with the water, as this again might cause the chocolate to become granular.

Put the egg whites into a bowl and pour the chocolate/butter mix over them. Using a wooden spatula, mix until thoroughly incorporated. This may take up to 5 minutes – if it is not mixed enough, the fondants may split. While incorporating the chocolate with the egg whites, try to do so with the minimum amount of air being added. This mixture will keep in the fridge until needed, although it is easier to fill the moulds while it is still warm.

To fill the moulds, first take some parchment paper and cut out strips that will fit around the inside of the rings without leaving any gaps. Butter the inside of the rings and one side of the paper strips. Line the inside of the rings with the paper, ensuring that the buttered side is facing inwards. Place each ring on a piece of buttered parchment paper, or stand the rings on butter paper, which will already be greased. Fill the moulds carefully with the mixture. If using ramekins, simply pour the mixture in.

Put the filled ring moulds or ramekins into the fridge for an hour or more. At this point they will keep well in the fridge for a couple of days. It is important to leave them to cool to fridge temperature, as the cooking time will be different if placed straight in the oven.

Place the rings in the preheated oven and cook for 6–8 minutes. Remove from the oven; the fondants should still look runny in the centre. The edges, however, should be slightly set; if not, leave the rings on for a minute or two, as they will continue to cook.

When they are ready, carefully slide a spatula underneath the fondants and lift each one on to a serving plate. Now carefully slide off each ring, taking care that the paper does not come off with it, and then, very gently, remove the strip of parchment. Do this slowly – if part of the fondant is stuck to the paper, you will need to ease it off with the point of a sharp knife. Although this sounds tricky, it will be easy having done the first one, believe me.

Although the fondants cannot be cooked in advance, a batch of mix can be ready in the fridge or the fondants could even be made up in advance and just cooked at the last minute.

The fondants should be left to stand for 3–4 minutes if using ring moulds, and 5–8 minutes if you using ramekins. The texture will then be just about perfect.

Probably the hardest thing with this recipe is to stop the children eating them while they are cooling down!

Hot Chocolate

The original Aztec chocolate drink was savoury, not sweet, and often combined with vanilla, chilli, pepper and even maize. It was not until much later that the drink became sweetened and synonymous with bedtime for children.

★ **Children's tip**

Try some of these experiments with your children – but they will only really work with the best bitter chocolate that you can find.

Finely chop a little chocolate and conduct a small 'tasting', using some of the savoury flavourings originally associated with chocolate. For example, try a piece of sweetcorn or a little ground pepper, maybe a tiny sprinkling of ground clove.

Try a little blue cheese! Yes, blue cheese. Not something like Roquefort, as that is a little salty. Something like Gorgonzola will be OK. Remember to keep an open mind. Get the children to taste the two together, in varying quantities and then one after the other in different order. Doing a little test with different cheeses could be great fun.

Tasting with your children will encourage them to keep an open mind.

It is very interesting to see how the brain will be telling us that, as this is a combination totally foreign to it and one that has always been a sweet one, we do not like it. If you and your children can try to detach your mind from these thoughts, you may well be pleasantly surprised. All in all, it just goes to show how much preconceived ideas influence what we like or dislike.

As adults, we are always telling our children that they must be more adventurous and try different foods instead of chips with everything. By doing this experiment ourselves, we adults might just understand the difficulty some younger children have in breaking some very early habits.

After all, we would not normally consider combining chocolate and blue cheese, but if we are able to dispel preconceived ideas and get the balance right, it really is a good combination.

Although there are only two ingredients in this recipe, the technique is a very old-fashioned one. It was used in the days when chocolate was very unstable and prone to splitting when only slightly heated. Nowadays lecithin is added to chocolate in order to make it more stable and able to withstand higher temperatures.

Whisking the milk improves the consistency and mouth-feel as the fat molecules clump together, giving it a richer and creamier characteristic.

To make about 4 mugs of hot chocolate
500ml whole milk
100g best-quality bitter chocolate, chopped

Using an electric whisk, beat the milk on a medium to high setting for 45 minutes. (This isn't a printing error; line the children up and let them take turns!)

Melt the chocolate in a bowl set over simmering water or in the microwave.

Once the milk has been whisked, pour it into a pan and bring it to the boil. As soon as this happens, pour the melted chocolate into the milk, simmer very gently for a few seconds until blended, and serve – that's it!

★ Children's tip

For as long as chocolate has been drunk, savoury or sweet, hot or cold, it has been prized for the quality of its froth. So much so that the Aztecs would pour it at height from one container to another just to obtain a foam. Later on, a form of swizzle-stick in a container was invented for the same purpose.

Using the pre-whisking technique in the recipe will leave a small natural foam – for a bit of fun, get the children to increase this by pouring the chocolate from one cup to another.

An even better method is a small, hand-held frother called an Aerolatte – it is not expensive and is a brilliant little gadget (see page 339). It incorporates air into soups, froths milk for coffees and gives great foam to your hot chocolate.

Hervé's Chocolate Chantilly

There really are very few new things in cooking and even fewer that are clever, simple and delicious. Hervé This, a French chemist with a Ph.D. in molecular gastronomy, came up with this a couple of years ago. This dish is so simple it defies belief. The only problem is that the chocolate needs to be hidden, or the children will be knocking this up all the time while your back is turned!

The dish basically uses the emulsification of the fat in the chocolate and the water to create what looks and tastes like chocolate-flavoured whipped cream. The beauty is, though, that there is no cream in it. This means that the pure taste of the chocolate comes through.

Chefs have long been told that water is the enemy of chocolate and, in some cases, it is, but it does not hold true for every recipe – as this shows.

A word of warning; the best-quality bitter chocolate does not mean the one with the highest percentage of cocoa solids (see page 297). These can sometimes taste powdery and bitter.

Makes 500g
230ml water
270g best-quality bitter chocolate

Break up the chocolate. Put it into a pan with the water and set it over a medium heat. Stir or whisk until the chocolate is completely melted.

It does not matter if the water boils, just make sure that it does not boil for long or some of the water will evaporate, altering the ratio of chocolate to water.

Have ready 2 bowls, one slightly larger than the other. Put some ice and cold water into the bigger bowl and place the smaller bowl in it. When the chocolate is completely melted, tip the mixture into the empty smaller bowl and with a balloon whisk or a hand-held electric whisk start beating. After a few minutes it should start to go like whipped cream.

Stop whisking just before you think it is ready, as it will thicken a little after. The beauty with this is that if you do over-whip it and it becomes grainy, then simply put it back on the heat to melt and start again.

If for some reason the mixture does not whip, there are two possibilities. First, there is too much water; simply add a little more chocolate and melt again. Second, it may be your whisk. If you see one of the offspring rosy-cheeked and out of breath, having no success, the whisk may not have enough wires and will therefore not work. I am speaking from bitter experience!

Some of the water could be substituted for, say, orange or passion fruit juice or, after the children are in bed, a splash of Calvados or malt whisky!

Rice Pudding

The technique for this is somewhere between a risotto and a rice pudding, and the result is more akin to a sweet risotto.

As a variation, lightly whip the cream before adding it, or just add a little whipped cream at the end.

This is a great basic recipe, one which can be adapted limitlessly. It can be a great way of getting the children to eat more fruit. As well as the obvious flavourings such as a little ground cinnamon or nutmeg, stir in macerated strawberries, or other red fruits. Bananas would work nicely. For a bit of decadence, make a chocolate rice pudding by stirring in some left-over hot chocolate.

Halve the vanilla pod lengthways and scrape out the seeds. Add the seeds and the pod to the milk, then bring to the boil and reduce the heat to a gentle simmer for 5 minutes. Remove from the heat and leave to infuse for half an hour.

Blanch the rice: bring 1 litre of water to the boil, add the rice, bring back to the boil, simmer for 3 minutes and drain; rinse under cold water.

Strain the milk through a fine sieve over the warm rice, add the sugar and nutmeg, and bring to the boil. Continue cooking on the boil until the rice is done, stirring almost continuously. This should take approximately half an

Serves 6

1 vanilla pod

750ml whole milk

135g Carnaroli or Arborio risotto rice

110g unrefined caster sugar

pinch of grated nutmeg

double cream (to taste: approximately 150ml)

2 egg yolks

orange-flower water (optional)

hour, but keep tasting the rice after 20 minutes. The cooking time will depend on the type of rice and your taste. Just remember that the grains do tend to harden a little when the rice has cooled down.

Once the rice is cooked there may be too much liquid. If so, just strain some of it off into a pan and reduce until it thickens sufficiently; likewise, if the rice is becoming too dry, just add a little more milk as required, bearing in mind that the rice will thicken as it cools and it may be necessary to add some more liquid if it is to be eaten cold. Leave the rice a little wet, as it will absorb more liquid while cooling down.

When the rice is ready, add the cream, cook for a couple of minutes more and remove from the heat (if whipping the cream, add it at the end). While the rice is still hot, add the egg yolks, and stir for 3 minutes off of the heat. Finish with the orange-flower water to taste.

If, when cold, the rice pudding seems too thick, simply stir in milk until the desired texture is achieved.

Flavourings such as cinnamon or cloves, or a little fruit purée or fruit, fresh or dried, can be added. Some strawberry juice (see page 294) would be delicious stirred in at the end.

Pears Poached in Red Wine

Although pears can be bought all year round, this has all the winter flavours in it, with some of the character of mulled wine, perfect for Christmas. As well as providing a sauce for the pears, the liquid can also make a lovely drink, hot or cold. Some of this liquid reduced down to a syrup can be poured over ice-cream or mixed into rice pudding.

Remember the saying: 'If the wine is not good enough to drink, do not cook with it.'

If you do not have any Crème de Cassis, use the same amount of blackcurrant syrup or add an extra 100g of sugar to the liquid. If the poaching liquid is a little thin, thicken it with a little cornflour.

These pears are always best made a day or two in advance. If they are eaten too soon, the poaching liquid will only have penetrated into some of the flesh, the centre part still being white.

★ Tip

As a chef, I was taught always to flame red wine before reducing it. This was apparently to minimize the acidity. Studies carried out recently, however, have shown that the measurement of acidity, pH, does not in fact change after flaming. This made me think: a teaspoon of vinegar will taste acidic – just try it on the kids and look at their faces! If, then, an equal measure of honey is added to the vinegar, its acidity (the pH) will not change; it will, however, taste less acidic. This means that its perceived acidity has changed.

We then carried out an experiment that can quite easily be done at home. Take 2 equal measurements of the same wine and put them in identical saucepans. If there are not 2 identical pans, heat one wine at a time. Bring the wines to the boil on the same heat so that they boil within seconds of each other.

As soon as the wine boils, ignite the wine in one pan and not the other. Leave the wine to boil until the flames have naturally died down. As soon as this happens, remove both of the wines from the heat. If doing one wine at a time, record the length of time that the wine flames for and allow the second wine to boil for that time too.

When both the wines have cooled down, taste them. Juggle the containers so that the kids don't know which wine is in what container. When they taste, try to get them to think about the acidity. When we did this it seemed that the acid levels in each were the some; however, the red wine that had not been flamed seemed to hold its acidity for longer, making it less palatable.

So, while it seems that flaming wine does not necessarily reduce the acidity, it does reduce the perceived acidity.

The ginger and liquorice are optional. If using liquorice, make sure that it is the dried root that you buy in a healthfood shop, not the confectionery.

You have a choice when preparing the pears: I think they look nicer left whole, but they are slightly more fiddly to prepare. If you haven't got the time or inclination for this, just cut them in half.

You will need a casserole large enough to hold the pears in one layer. You may have to adjust the quantities accordingly, depending on how many pears you can fit into the pan.

Bring the wine to the boil, flame it, and add all of the other ingredients except the pears. Be patient and allow the flames to die down on their own. When the flames have gone, remove the pan from the heat.

Meanwhile, peel the pears. If keeping them whole, remove the core so that they will cook evenly the whole way through. Insert the tip of a peeler into the base of the pear just on the edge of the core, push it into the fruit, and turning the peeler around the core, cut it out. If halving the pears, do so lengthways and use the tip of the peeler to cut out the root and the core.

The liquid will now have cooled down a little. Place the pears side by side, standing upright if whole. Top with a cartouche (see page 50), pressing down slightly so that some of the poaching liquid comes through the holes made in the paper, to keep the pears submerged during cooking. Use a casserole just big enough to hold the pears in in one layer. The liquid should completely cover the pears, but if it doesn't, simply top up with just enough water to cover them.

Put the casserole back on the heat and bring the liquid to a simmer. Turn the heat down and cook at a very gentle simmer, just enough to form the odd bubble on the surface of the water. Cook the pears until they are done; test this by inserting a small pointed knife into the flesh. If it goes in with little resistance, they are ready. Timings will vary quite noticeably, depending on the type of pear and its ripeness. Between 10 and 20 minutes is a rough guideline.

Serves 6–8

8–10 ripe and unblemished pears such as Conference (allow 1–2 pears per person)

1 bottle of red wine

200ml Crème de Cassis or blackcurrant syrup (if not available, use an extra 100g sugar)

200g sugar

1 cinnamon stick

6 cloves

1 star anise

20g fresh ginger, peeled and thinly sliced

2 sticks of liquorice root

zest of 1 orange and 1 lemon (remove this in large pieces using a potato peeler)

Remove the pan from the heat and leave to cool. When cold, carefully transfer the fruit to a sealable container and store in the fridge for at least 1 day. The pears will keep for a week in the poaching liquid.

Serve hot or cold, adjusting the consistency of the liquid as required – add water if too thick, boil to reduce if too thin.

Basil Bavarois (Blanc Manger)

Blanc manger is a French classic, white and creamy, a real childhood dessert, quite different from the maligned pink stodgy version known in this country. Traditionally, this classic dessert is made with almonds and is set with gelatine. The name means 'white food', and referred to a dessert in the Middle Ages made from white chicken or veal meat and flavoured with honey and almonds (maybe just a step too far for your children).

Bavarois is similar, but does not necessarily contain almonds. It is made by setting cream or custard, such as the one made for the vanilla ice-cream, with gelatine. Lightly whipped cream is then folded in. It can be flavoured to taste.

It's a very easy dessert to make. It is delicious made with really good-quality fromage blanc, as it lends a delicate acidity to the dish. It can be made without fromage blanc, substituting cream or even some mascarpone, but I don't recommend using anything like Greek yoghurt.

Using the unrefined sugar in this recipe lessens the whiteness of the dessert but more than compensates in flavour. The basil gives this dish a wonderful flavour and great colour. Please do not balk at the amount!

The bavarois must be made the day before it is to be served it, otherwise it will not have enough time to set.

Halve the vanilla pod, scrape out the seeds and set aside. Place the gelatine leaves in a bowl of cold water until they are soft (about 5 minutes). If using fromage blanc, mix it with the sugar in a bowl.

Meanwhile, put the vanilla seeds into a pan with the milk; bring to a light simmer and remove from the heat. If using all double cream rather than fromage blanc, add the sugar to the milk now. Squeeze the water out of the gelatine and add to the hot but not boiling milk, whisking until dissolved. Pass through a fine-meshed sieve.

Bring a large pot of water to the boil and have ready a large bowl of iced or cold water. Plunge the basil leaves into the hot water for 10 seconds, then remove and immediately plunge them into the cold water. Drain the leaves and thoroughly pat dry between tea towels or kitchen paper.

Put all the double cream into a cold bowl and whisk until it begins to thicken and just holds when the whisk is lifted up from the bowl. It is very important that the cream is not over-whisked, or it will become grainy.

Liquidize the basil leaves with the cooled milk for a couple of minutes. Strain through muslin or the finest sieve available. Mix in the fromage blanc and fold in the whisked cream. Pour into a bowl or individual ramekins and leave in the fridge until set.

To serve, dip the bowl or mould in hot water for a few seconds, cover with the plate that it will be served on and quickly turn it upside down.

Serves 4

1 vanilla pod

2¹/₂ leaves of gelatine

185g fromage blanc (or the same amount of double cream)

45g unrefined caster sugar

90g whole milk

325g fresh basil leaves

90g double cream

★ **Children's tip**

Turning out the bavarois is something the children will definitely want to do, but just watch them. We had World War Three over who was going to do this, resulting in a nice new kitchen floor!

This would be delicious served with the pears poached in red wine (page 307).

Crumble

There had to be a recipe for crumble in this book – one of this country's most famous desserts and definitely one that we have all grown up with. Although the most popular form of crumble is obviously apple, just about any fruit can be used.

Here are two crumble recipes. The first is the more simple, classic one that is put on top of the fruit and requires 10–15 minutes in the oven to cook it. The second is a recipe that is precooked and will stay crunchy, stored in an airtight container for several days. This one can be sprinkled over fruits such as strawberries, giving a wonderful textural contrast. The beauty of this second recipe is that the whole family will always have something to hand to turn a bowl of fruit into a dessert.

Salt plays an essential role in the flavour of a crumble; don't be shy with it.

Classic Crumble

The quantity of crumble needed depends on the surface area of your baking dish and how thick you want the topping to be. It's very easy to remember. Simply take equal quantities of the following:

unrefined caster sugar
butter
ground almonds
flour
Approximately 100g of each, plus 1 teaspoon of salt, should be sufficient for 4–6 hungry people.

Combine the sugar and butter in a bowl with the ground almonds. Sieve the flour over, add 1 teaspoon of salt, and work the mixture with your fingertips until it forms large granules of dough; reserve in the fridge until needed.

To use, first preheat the oven to 200°C/gas mark 6. Spread the crumble mixture over the fruit in the oven dish and bake for 10–15 minutes or until lightly browned on top.

Crunchy Crumble

225g unsalted butter

175g plain flour

140g unrefined caster sugar

100g ground almonds

gingerbread (you can use any spiced bread obtainable from the supermarket – the German spiced breads work well in this recipe, as does Jamaica ginger cake)

salt

Preheat the oven to 180°C/gas mark 4.

Make a beurre noisette with the butter as described in the recipe for braised lettuces (page 207).

Combine all the ingredients in a food processor and reduce to crumbs. If a food processor is not available, use the children's fingertips.

Cover a large baking tray with parchment paper, spread the crumble mix on top, and put into the preheated oven. Every 10–15 minutes, turn the mixture over until it becomes golden brown and crunchy. Be careful not to cook is too long – the mix will already be a brown colour due to the spiced bread.

Leave to cool before storing.

Crumble Bases

Here are two examples of a fruit base for crumble. The first is more suited for the classic crumble topping and the second to the precooked crunchy crumble.

Compote of Apples with Raisins

Halve the vanilla pod lengthways, scrape out the seeds and reserve. (Keep the pod for another use, or dry it and infuse in your sugar pot.)

Peel, halve and core the apples. Cut them into 1cm dice. Sauté them in the butter, keeping the pan at a temperature that maintains the butter at a golden brown colour. After 2 minutes, add the cinnamon, the raisins and the Calvados, if using, and cook for a further 3 minutes. Remove from the heat.

To finish the dish, put the apple compote into an ovenproof dish, cover with the classic crumble and bake at 200°C/gas mark 6 for 10–15 minutes.

Serves 2

1 vanilla pod
3 Braeburn or Cox apples
75g unsalted butter
a little ground cinnamon
50g raisins
25ml Calvados (optional)

Rhubarb Crumble/Compote

This is better suited to the pre-made crumble, as rhubarb cooks very quickly and will become soft and mushy in no time at all.

Macerating the rhubarb in the sugar makes a world of difference in intensifying the flavour. If you do not have the time or inclination to macerate the rhubarb for 2 days, a couple of hours will still help.

20 stems of rhubarb
100g unrefined caster sugar
50g unsalted butter

Top and tail the rhubarb stems and peel them with a small sharp knife. Cut them into 2–3cm lengths, put into a bowl, and mix in all but 3 teaspoons of the sugar. Leave for 2 hours, or up to 2 days.

In a frying pan large enough to hold all the rhubarb in one layer, heat the butter until it is hot and foaming. Add the rhubarb and any juice that has come out of it, and cook gently for 10 minutes. If the rhubarb will not fit in the pan in one large layer, cook it in batches.

This compote will keep well for a couple of days in the fridge.

To serve, put the compote into a baking dish, reheat in the oven, and sprinkle over the precooked topping. The purée can also be heated in a pan and served with the crumble on the side in a bowl for people to help themselves.

Confiture de Lait (Milk Jam)

This is a very traditional French childhood taste. It is very simple to make and is delicious on toast or with ice-cream. The children will not be able to resist it.

1 litre whole milk
1 vanilla pod
500g unrefined caster sugar

Put the milk in a casserole. Halve the vanilla pod lengthways and scrape out the seeds. Add the seeds and pod to the milk. Add the sugar and very gently bring the milk to the boil. Simmer very gently, stirring from time to time.

After a couple of hours, the milk will begin to thicken and turn golden brown. It is important that as this starts to happen it should be stirred as often as possible.

Remove the vanilla pod as the mixture thickens and stir continuously. This is very important for the texture and to stop the mix from catching.

When the mixture has thickened and is light caramel in colour, it is ready. Tip the contents of the pan into a liquidizer and blend on full power for a couple of minutes until completely smooth. Pour into a big pot or individual ramekins and leave in the fridge for a week before serving.

★ **Tip**
A short cut: place an unopened tin of condensed milk in a pressure cooker, fill the cooker one third with water, and cook under pressure for 1 hour. Make sure that the tin is left to cool completely before opening.

Biscuit

A book on family cooking had to contain a biscuit recipe. This is a very interesting one, as the word effectively means 'twice-cooked'; and this is exactly what this biscuit recipe is.

These biscuits are wonderfully crumbly.

Makes 20–30 biscuits
For the first stage
190g plain flour
110g ground almonds
75g icing sugar
110g unsalted butter
a good pinch of salt
For the second stage
75g unsalted butter

Preheat the oven to 170°C/gas mark 3.

Combine the first 4 ingredients together, mixing with your fingertips until a sandy texture develops. Spread this mixture out on to a baking sheet lined with greaseproof paper. The sheet should be sufficiently large for the mix to be no more than 1cm deep. Bake in the preheated oven for about 25 minutes. Every 5 minutes, open the oven door and 'rake over' the mix. This will ensure even cooking.

The mixture is ready when it has taken on a dry whiteness, meaning that the dough has, basically, been cooked but not taken on any colour.

For the second stage, tip the crumbly dough into a food processor and add the remaining 75g of butter, in pieces, at room temperature. Process until the mixture forms a uniform mass. Spread back on to the baking sheet again. Place another sheet of greaseproof paper on top, then roll or flatten the dough to a thickness of between 1 and 2cm and put back into the oven (still at the same temperature).

At this stage do not panic – the dough will be a crumbly mass, which is how it is meant to be. Cook until lightly golden – roughly 20 minutes.

When ready, remove from the oven and, with a circular cutter, the size of your choice, cut out the biscuits. It is important to do this while it is still hot, otherwise, as it cools down, the biscuit base will harden and crumble. If you do not have any cutters, cut the biscuit with a knife.

Some crystallized sugar sprinkled over the biscuits works well.

Salted Butter Caramels

These are a speciality of Brittany, although many countries around the world have their own version. This recipe cheats a little by using unsalted butter with the addition of salt instead of salted butter.

At the Fat Duck we make a larger version of this and serve it with a chocolate and thyme sorbet and a cumin caramel sauce (see page 324). It's a bit like the inside of a Snickers bar.

The recipe is relatively simple to make and will keep for a couple of weeks in the fridge. The characteristic flavour comes mainly from the salt and the reaction between the sugar and the protein in the milk while cooking.

The two most important factors here are that unfortunately the mix must be stirred continually for the duration of the cooking time, making sure that all the corners and edges of the pan are covered, and second, that the caramel is left in the pan overnight before storing. If not, it will split or become grainy.

With a little experience, however, you will be able to make this perfectly each time, and a thermometer will make the recipe almost foolproof. Make sure that you have a casserole large enough; the mixture should be no deeper than 5cm.

Finally, take care as you whisk; the mixture gets very hot!

This recipe will make quite a lot, so, although it keeps well (if it has the chance!), it may be an idea to halve the recipe ingredients.

Preheat the oven to 180°C/gas mark 4.

375g unrefined caster sugar

375g liquid glucose

375g whole milk

300g best-quality unsalted butter

10g salt

450g whipping cream

150g peeled pistachios (if you cannot get hold of peeled pistachios, leave them out, otherwise you will never forgive me for telling you to peel them!)

150g salted peanuts

Combine all the ingredients except the whipping cream and the nuts in a casserole and put on a high heat, whisking continuously with a balloon whisk. It is very important not to stop whisking and that the corners and sides of the pan do not get ignored. Unfortunately, this will take up to 45 minutes.

If you have a thermometer, or a probe (see page 26), take the mixture to 120°C. If you do not have one, cook until the caramel is a light brown colour, a little darker than the inside of a Snickers bar. As a slightly more accurate guideline, the mixture will be ready when it begins to split and comes together as one slippery mass.

Now, off the heat, pour in the whipping cream and mix as hard as possible (forget going to the gym today!). Make sure that the caramel is really well mixed. Stir for a further 5 minutes.

Roast the nuts in the oven for 10 minutes or until brown, taking care not to overcook them. Stir into the mixture.

Now leave overnight so that the texture can improve (it will harden up). It can then be stored in the fridge for a couple of weeks.

Cumin Caramel Sauce

This is the sauce that accompanies the Salted Butter Caramels at the restaurant. It is delicious, easy to make, and will keep for quite a long time in a sealed container in the fridge.

This sauce has a multitude of uses, ranging from drizzling over ice-cream to mixing with rice pudding.

Just be careful when making the caramel and adding the butter; it is very hot.

Blitz the cinnamon sticks in a blender and put into a casserole along with the cumin seeds. Dry-fry on a medium heat for a couple of minutes until the mix becomes aromatic. Pour over the cream and, as soon as it comes to the boil, turn the heat down so that the cream simmers for 2 minutes. Turn off the heat and leave to infuse for half an hour. (If you do not have any cinnamon sticks, replace them with a tablespoon of powdered cinnamon.)

1½ cinnamon sticks
½ heaped tablespoon cumin seeds
100g unrefined caster sugar
40g unsalted butter, cubed
100g double cream

Have ready a brush and a cup of cold water. Pour the sugar into another casserole and place on a medium heat. Do not stir the sugar, but brush cold water around the edge of the pan. This helps to prevent sugar crystallizing around the edge of the pan and burning in the corners. Be careful, as unrefined sugar has a lower water content and caramelizes very quickly.

As soon as a dark caramel is reached, add the butter. To be on the safe side, wrap a tea-towel round your hand to ensure that any caramel bubbling over (it shouldn't) will not do damage. You can now stir the mix.

When blended, pour over the warm cream (still containing the spices), simmer for 3 minutes, then pass the mixture through a fine-meshed sieve. It is now ready to use.

★ **Children's tip**
This sauce can be made without any flavouring to begin with and experimented with afterwards. I am quite sure that your children will not mind this at all!

Mrs Blumenthal's Cheesecake

There are two childhood kitchen-related experiences which I will never forget. The first is being shouted at for having jumped up and down long enough to break the seal on the pressure cooker with the chicken broth in it. The second was not being able to wait for the whole day that the cheesecake had to rest before being eaten!

This book would not be complete without one of my mother's recipes.

Makes enough to fill a 25cm springform cake tin
75g unsalted butter
12 digestive biscuits
1 level coffeespoon salt
375g full-fat cottage cheese
375g best-quality cream cheese
5 whole eggs
1 teaspoon vanilla extract
210g sour cream
65g cornflour
160g caster sugar

Preheat the oven to 150°C/gas mark 2.

Melt 65g of the butter in a small saucepan and remove from the heat. Using either a food processor or a rolling-pin and a plastic bag, crush the biscuits until fine. By hand, mix in the melted butter and add the salt.

Use the remaining 10g of butter to grease the cake tin, and spread the biscuit mix over the base, pressing down firmly so that it forms a compact, even layer.

Now, rub the cottage cheese through a fine mesh sieve using the back of a ladle or spoon. A vegetable mill or ricer will work quite well for this. Add the cream cheese and mix well.

Separate the eggs. Put the whites into a large mixing bowl. Beat the egg yolks into the cheese mixture and add the vanilla extract. Stir in the sour cream. Sieve the cornflour over this and mix.

Add the sugar to the egg whites and whisk to a soft peak. Mix a third of the egg white into the cheese mixture to loosen it, then delicately fold in the rest of the egg whites.

Pour on top of the biscuit base in the greased cake tin.

Cook for 1 hour and 15 minutes in the preheated oven. Turn the oven off and leave until cold. This cake will rise and then fall again during cooking.

When cold, remove from the cake tin and serve. This can be made the night before serving.

Jack's Raspberry Crunch

This is where my son, Jack, lets his creativity and ability to generate chaos go wild! The end result is either a drinkable dessert or something that has the texture of mashed-up ice-cream with a crunch. It really does depend on what ingredients children use or have to hand and, well, on the mood at the time!

The whole point is that the kids make this up as they go along, sieving, crushing, mixing and tasting; oh, and of course, messing!

A word of warning; do not ask them to make this if you are relying on it as a dessert. They will end up eating most of it before finishing!

a couple of small tubs of fresh raspberries (or the equivalent in frozen raspberries)

about half of the quantity of this in raspberry juice (fresh fruit juice mixes work well)

a scoop of the following ice creams: raspberry, chocolate, vanilla

3 of each of the following biscuits: chocolate chip cookies, ginger biscuits, orange or lemon biscuits

Purée the raspberries (defrosted if frozen) in a liquidizer or with a hand blender. Force through a fine sieve with the back of a spoon into a clean bowl.

If using a liquidizer, wash it out and put the purée back into it. Add the raspberry juice and blend. Add the ice-creams and blend again until thoroughly mixed.

Now, crush the biscuits. Without a doubt, the best way to do this is with a rolling-pin as it is the most fun, makes a lot of noise and produces sufficient mess!

The little chefs can now add or adjust as they feel fit or their taste guides them.

When ready, either serve in a glass or bowl, depending on the texture that you end up with, or do as Jack prefers – return it to the freezer and leave until nice and cold.

★ **Variation**

The raspberries can be replaced with any fruit. Strawberries or bananas, for example, will work well. The ice creams and biscuits can also be varied to taste.

Although the above recipe is Jack's, the whole point of this is that the children can really let themselves go. Don't interfere with their creativity here!

Glossary

Blanch: Refers to food that has been plunged into boiling water and then into iced water. It is a technique that is used for various things, ranging from precooking vegetables to loosening the skin of fruits. There are a couple of variations. In recipes that require meat to be blanched it is placed into cold water and brought to the boil. The meat is then drained off and put back into fresh water. This helps to rid it of some of its impurities. Blanch also refers to the process of whisking egg yolks and sugar together until the mix whitens. Used in the making of custards and ice-creams.

Boil: Boil is a word that is still misused. You may be wondering why it is included in this glossary. Water boils at 100°C at sea level. Too often, a recipe will advise bringing the water to a rolling boil or to a strong boil; water itself either boils or it doesn't. There are exceptions to this. However, although water boils at 100°C, other ingredients often mixed with it do boil at higher temperatures. When making sugar syrup, for example, the recipe will tell you to bring the sugar and water to the boil and take the syrup to 121°C. Here, although the water turns to steam and evaporates at 100°C, the sugar in the mix will allow the temperature to increase beyond 100°C.

Bouquet garni: A term referring to a mixture of herbs often wrapped in a strip of leek and tied with string into a bundle. A standard bouquet garni will consist of thyme, bay leaf, parsley and celery leaves, although it will vary depending on the type of dish being prepared. Although recipes will always tell you to tie the bundle of herbs up, this is only necessary if they all need to be removed from the dish at some point.

Caramelize: Whenever a recipe tells you to caramelize something, it will intend that you brown it in varying degrees. The process is a very complicated one and involves breaking down mainly sugars and starches with heat until they become golden or brown and develop a rich taste. Please note that caramelization is not involved in toasting bread; this involves dextrins, starch molecules that have been altered by heat. It is useful to know that the stage after caramelization is normally burnt!

Cartouche: A perforated cover, usually made from parchment paper, that sits on the surface of a liquid containing solid matter. For example, it helps to keep fruits that are to be poached submerged in the liquid while allowing steam to escape.

Coagulation: In the kitchen, this refers to the toughening or cooking of proteins. It is most visible in egg cookery. Eggs scramble because of the proteins coagulating (they clump together). Coagulation is also responsible for making custard, as it is partial coagulation that causes the eggs to thicken the liquid.

Core: The removal of the middle of a fruit or vegetable and with it its seeds and in the case of, say, red pepper, the pith too. The technique varies depending on the type of fruit or vegetable and the way that it will be used in the dish itself.

Deglaze: The process of adding a little liquid, normally water, to a pan containing concentrated, browned juices that have stuck to the pan and scraping to free them. This liquid can then be added to the other ingredients or may form the basis of a sauce. It is an essential way of concentrating the flavours in a dish. Many of these flavours may well be caused by the Maillard reaction (q.v.).

Deseed: This just refers to removing the seeds from a fruit, such as a passion fruit or tomato (remember, anything housing its seeds on the inside is a fruit). The process normally involves halving the fruit and scooping out the seeds.

Lardons: Lardons are traditionally belly or back fat of pork, cut into rectangles and used to keep a piece of meat moist during cooking (the fat would gently melt as the meat cooks). This word is now used for pieces of bacon as well and for pieces of meat cut into this shape and used for, among other things, salad and pasta garnishes.

Liquidize: Refers specifically to an ingredient or mix of ingredients that will be reduced to some form of liquid, usually by putting into a blender or liquidizer.

Maillard reaction: Maillard reactions are responsible for most of the browned roasting flavours that we like to eat and are some of the most complex reactions in the kitchen. This reaction essentially involves sugars being browned in the presence of amino acids. The reaction is named after the Frenchman who first intentionally heated amino acids in a high glucose solution. Although these reactions are very often desirable – on the outside of a piece of meat or in toffee – they are sometimes unwanted, as in the leek and potato soup recipe or in scrambled egg.

Mouli: These old-fashioned vegetable mills are still very useful for puréeing vegetables, mashed potatoes for example. If you decide to buy one, the bigger 25cm diameter ones are far more useful than the more readily available little ones.

Pass: The word used in the kitchen for straining a liquid through a sieve or muslin, or forcing a purée through a sieve to make it finer.

Poach: A term used very loosely to describe, nearly always, protein-based foods that are to be cooked in liquid maintained below boiling point. The temperature for poaching is not really definable, although it generally refers to temperatures below that used when simmering.

Pod: A pod is the outside casing of a bean, whether it be a pea, broad bean, fresh haricot bean (white or green) or vanilla (all of these are, technically, fruits). To pod something refers to the removal of this casing to get to the beans or peas inside.

Process: To put a mixture, solid or liquid, into a blender to break it down.

Reduce: This word usually refers to boiling a liquid so that its quantity is reduced and the flavour of the liquid itself is intensified. Sometimes it will be required to reduce a liquid to dry, i.e. vinegar. It can also be related to food that is to be processed: for example, reduced to a purée.

Refresh: Refreshing is the process of plunging an ingredient, usually vegetables or herbs, into a container of iced water to stop it from cooking any more.

Sauté: For the purpose of this book, this refers to ingredients being fried, more aggressively than sweating, for a relatively short space of time. The word means 'jump' in French and refers to the ingredients being tossed around in the pan. It also refers to a type of dish – a 'sauté' – meaning that the dish is prepared in the same pan and is cooked by frying.

Season: Adding salt and pepper for the purpose of flavour enhancement. The pepper should always be freshly ground, whether from a mill or done in a pestle and mortar.

Simmer: As mentioned earlier, water boils at 100°C. From 96 to 99°C the water will be simmering. You will notice the difference between the two temperatures. The ingredient and the nature of the dish itself will determine the level of simmering required.

Skim: The process of removing the impurities, or fat, from the surface of a liquid. A useful technique for this is to take a ladle, dip it partially into the liquid, and, starting from the centre, make a spiralling movement towards the edge. By doing this, most of the unwanted bits from the surface of the liquid will be transferred to the edge of the pan. Then, using the ladle, tilted with one side in contact with the inside of the pan, move around the edge, collecting the fat or scum as you go.

Stud: Often used to describe pushing cloves into an onion when making soups, stocks or sauces. It is also used for inserting other ingredients into meat, such as garlic into the pork in the pot-roast pork recipe (page 153) or lardons into meat, game or fish.

Sweat: This is the process of gently frying vegetables in a small amount of fat (usually oil) until translucent. They will give out their initial moisture (hence the term).

Top and tail: This is the process of removing the ends of green beans, traditionally done by hand. It can be done with a knife, trimming off both ends, although when using larger or tougher beans, they will need to be done by hand. As the end is snapped off, the stringy part running along the edge of the bean will still be attached to it, enabling it to be pulled off.

Unrefined sugar: In this book, the term 'unrefined' refers to the sugar that I use almost exclusively at the Fat Duck and which is now widely available in all of the big supermarkets.

Because the sugar has not gone through the refining process it is not white in colour and has a faint smell of molasses. Its flavour is full of childhood memories! It is important to know that unrefined sugar contains less water. This means that it will caramelize very quickly. This can be very useful when making the crust for, say, a crème brûlée, as the sugar will caramelize so quickly that the delicate cream underneath will not overheat. The sugar will, however, turn from caramel to burnt relatively quickly.

Useful Addresses

This list does not include specialist food suppliers – the book is for people both in England and abroad, and one of the points that it tries to make is that by understanding some of the principles and techniques used in the kitchen you can turn everyday ingredients into something special. The important thing is always to seek out the best-quality produce that you can lay your hands on.

Equipment

You can find what you need in most kitchen shops and department stores, but Hansens will supply all the equipment mentioned in this book and they offer a mail order service. Their address is:

Hansens
306 Fulham Road
London SW10 9ER
www.hansens.co.uk

In particular, I cannot recommend strongly enough the importance of the following pieces of equipment:

Digital probe or thermometer These are more accurate than the more traditional meat thermometers and are worth their weight in gold.

Oven thermometer You will be amazed just how inaccurate many ovens are, even the most expensive. Recipes that you think have failed because of something you did wrong or a fault in the recipe itself may in fact have been unsuccessful because of your oven!

Japanese slicer or mandoline These can be expensive, but the cheaper plastic Japanese slicers are just as good and about five times less expensive.

Knives Hansens sell what I consider to be the best available, MAC. These are not cheap but are simply the best!

Hygiene

Hygiene in the kitchen is vital, and something that we should all be aware of. The Food Standards Agency will be able to answer any questions that you may have and they have a website. Their address is:

Food Standards Agency
Aviation House
125 Kingsway
London WC2B 6NH
www.food.gov.uk

The Fat Duck

Finally, if you are interested in finding out a little more about the Fat Duck, please visit the website at *www.fatduck.co.uk*

Index

garlic
  Confit Garlic 196–7
  inserting into lamb 174
  purée: Carbonara 84–6
  Risotto 94
  wine 65
Gazpacho 121–6
ginger
  Braised Lentils 238–41
  Pears Poached in Red Wine
    307–10
gingerbread: Crumble 315
glaze for Pot-roast Pork 155, 157
Glazed Carrots 212–13
grains
  Basic Pasta Dough 89–91
  Carbonara 84–6
  Couscous 108–12
  Gratin of Macaroni 87–8
  Risotto 92–107
Gratin of Macaroni 87–8
Gratin of Potatoes 222–4
gravy see sauces
green beans see haricot beans
grilling fish 264–5
gruyère cheese: Gratin of Macaroni
    87–8

hand washing, importance 148
hard water problems 74
haricot beans 75
  Baked Beans 76–8
  Haricots à la Crème 205
  Salad of Haricots Verts 204
hay cooking 162–4

hazelnuts: Couscous with Hazelnuts
    and Rosemary 110
herbs
  Beef Juice 172–3
  Braised Shoulder of Lamb 181–3
  Carbonara 84–6
  in crushed potatoes 220
  Vegetables en Cocotte 248–9
  wine 65
  see also specific herbs and bouquet
    garnis
Hervé's Chocolate Chantilly 303–4
horseradish in gratin of potatoes
    224
Hot Chocolate 300–302
hygiene 22–3, 148, 159

ice-cream machine 279
ice-creams 279
  Jack's Raspberry Crunch 328–9
  Vanilla Ice-cream 280–82
infusing 101

Jack's Raspberry Crunch 328–9
jelly, beetroot 31–2
juice drinks 14
jus 153–4

ketchup, tomato 50–52
kneading 163
knives 25

La Côte Saint Jacques 121
lamb
  Braised Shoulder of Lamb 181–3

buying 174
Roast Leg of Lamb 174–6
Seven-hour Leg of Lamb 177–80
leeks
  Beef Juice 172–3
  Braised Lentils 238–41
  Braised Oxtail 184–9
  Chicken Soup 134–7
  Leek and Potato Soup 127–9
  Lentil Soup 132–4
  Pot-roast Pork 153–7
lemon: Strawberry Soup 293–6
lemongrass: Chicken Soup 136
lentils
  Braised Lentils 238–42
  buying 238
  cooking 239
  Lentil Purée 243
  Lentil Soup 132–4
lettuce
  Braised Lettuces 207–9
  Vegetables en Cocotte 248–9
  liquidizers 24, 117, 128–9
liquorice: Pears Poached in Red
    Wine 307–10
local traders 12
Loiseau, Bernard 60
low temperature cooking 144–7
  Braised Oxtail 184–9
  fish 264–5
  Roast Wing Rib of Beef 171
  Seven-hour Leg of Lamb 177–80

macaroni: Gratin of Macaroni 87–8
mackerel: topping 68